# THE
# NOW
# GOLFER

## THE PSYCHOLOGY OF
## BETTER GOLF

By

## Dr. Preston Waddington

With
## Don Lay

WWW.NOWGOLFER.COM

# DEDICATION

For my wife Barbara, with whom
the sun rises and the sun sets - Pres

# TABLE OF CONTENTS

## PART 1

# PART 2

# FOREWORD BY STEWART CINK

---

*Golf is simply a contest to determine who
can get out of their own way the most often.*

---

I have always been a golfer. Since before memory began,
the game has been part of my life. I started around age
two, tagging along with my parents when they went out
to the local muni. I didn't so much learn the game from
them, as I learned to love the game. I had the passion to
improve every day and I loved the process. Playing my
first tournament at age eight, I was the winner. I was able
to become the top player in each age group along the way,
finally becoming the top junior golfer in the nation at age
17. My goal of earning a college scholarship was fulfilled,
and I enrolled at Georgia Tech in 1991. A small fish in a
big pond, once again I was able to rise to the top of the
ranks by my senior year, and finished my college career
with national Player of the Year honors.

Degree in hand, a dominant year in golf's minor league
only affirmed my career was headed in the right direction,
and full of promise. As a rookie on the PGA Tour in 1997,
I didn't skip a beat. Experiencing almost immediate success, I was a winner that season in Hartford and was named
Rookie of the Year. The sun was shining brightly and there
was no limit to where my career may go.

But there was something happening of which I was unaware. It was slowly creeping into my subconscious. Having been a golfer, and a successful one, my whole life, I had unknowingly begun to tie my golf performance into my own sense of self-identity. I had probably always done it to a certain extent, but a few things had changed since I became a professional. First, my expectations had continued to grow unbridled. Through my own successes, I had convinced myself that I should only be successful. My expectations were high. As my career began on the PGA Tour, the golf courses had become more exacting, and competition was deeper than I had ever seen before. Naturally I was experiencing more little failures, falling short of my own expectations. Secondly, after winning as a rookie in 1997, I began to put pressure on myself to live up to some lofty standard I had created for myself. In my mind I now needed to carry the mantle of being a winner on the PGA Tour.

Acceptance of and self-forgiveness for mistakes had slowly become a thing of the past. Three putts, balls hit into penalty situations, over par rounds, are all normal experiences in the game. However, because of my high level of expectations, I had allowed each bad result to become an assault on my sense of self-worth. It was like I was hiding some kind of secret that was inevitably going to be revealed. Golf became not a game at all, but a challenge to keep my failures under wraps so no one could see.

It happened so slowly, over the course of many years, that I failed to even notice. But my thought patterns had become professionally debilitating, and I was dreading each and every day of competition.

In 2002, I had taken notice of my situation, and I decided something needed to be done. At the time, my swing coach and friend, Mark Wood, recommended I speak to Preston Waddington, a psychoanalyst and golfer at the club in Florida where I practiced with my coach. I was hesitant to move forward, invoking my tendency to want to hide what I perceived as weakness. When I finally decided to take the step and visit with Preston, I vowed to be fully transparent and not hide from any topics.

I'll always remember that first conversation. Speaking about myself in this way for the first time, I felt like a weight had been thrown from my shoulders! Of course, it was only the very beginning, and over the past ten years, Preston has helped me strip away the layers of grime and rust that I had allowed to accumulate. I have learned about myself in ways I would never have otherwise. Throughout our relationship, the goal for me has always been better golf, but I have noticed a sweeter change–a better life. Acceptance of poor results does not substitute for intense focus and commitment. For while mistake free golf will never exist, those mistakes are now so much more acceptable for what they are, simply part of the game that every player has to come to terms with. That level of acceptance has allowed me to unlock my potential–that is, my potential to be at peace with whatever I do on and off the golf course.

My work with Preston has allowed me to be more efficient at practice, and a better husband and father.
But most of all, it's helped me to get out of my own way.
Stewart Cink, August 2012.

# ABOUT THIS BOOK

W.C. Fields, the renowned comedian and film star, once sat on the golf course in a total funk after yet another disastrous round. Bobby Jones, seeing that his friend had basically given up on the game of golf, tried to console him.

" It can't be that bad."

" It's worse," W.C. quipped, " And you don't deserve any credit, hitting the ball with that swing of yours. Try to hit one with my swing."

W.C. FIELDS

W.C. Fields had a point. Not everyone can have the graceful and powerful swing of a legend like Bobby Jones. Each player has his own unique swing, his own unique style.

This book is about hitting the ball with your swing.

Unlike almost every golf book ever written, there are no mechanical instructions contained herein. There are no chapters on how to hold your grip, adjust your swing plane, or change the length of your backswing. There are no equipment recommendations or instructions about your stance. For this technical information we need only peruse the endless books available on the subject, or better yet seek the advice of a local teaching professional.

The Now Golfer is about maximizing the outcome of the swing you already possess, and about improving scores and gaining results without external mechanical adjustments.

This book is about recognizing the mental and emotional processes occurring within one's Self on the golf course and how to regulate them.

Dr. Preston Waddington has advised a wide range of golfers, from the club player to top-level pros like Players Champion Tim Clark and British Open Champion Stewart Cink, among others. Waddington's expertise, once available to the few, is now available to the many in this concise volume.

The chapters were intentionally kept short so that the reader can absorb the maximum amount of information in a minimum amount of reading time. The chapter titles refer to concepts that can be revisited so The Now Golfer can also be used as a reference book. Illustrations and vintage photos complement the text and help to reinforce the message.

Important concepts and terms are capitalized, italicized, or both. For the sake of continuity the common pronoun "he" is used to represent both genders. Although I write some portions of this book in the first person, all of the theories and concepts come from Pres Waddington. It is my privilege to write his words.

Don Lay, June 2012

# THE MELTDOWN

Alex is a pro golfer who has been playing on the tour for three years. As a junior he won most of the tournaments he played in and later on did well playing college golf. After turning pro he fought his way up the ranks to qualify for major tournaments and has had some top ten finishes.

Now, on the final day of this PGA tour event, he finds himself one-up as he readies his approach shot on eighteen. He has played well all week and today was his best day, linking together a long string of pars and birdies. He stands over his shot and launches a beautiful wedge onto the green, landing twenty-seven inches from the hole. Alex raises his arms above his head in celebration as the gallery enthusiastically shows its appreciation.

On the walk to the green, Alex can feel a flood of emotions inside, for this will be his first PGA tournament victory. Who wouldn't be proud? As he crosses the green to his shot he feels the emotions inside of him shift into a strange and uncomfortable energy. A numbing sensation starts in his arms and legs. Against his will, his heart begins to pound in his chest and his respiration becomes irregular. His normally fluid muscles involuntarily tighten, and as every camera around the green focuses on him, he stands over his putt. He needs only to sink it to win.

It is such a simple putt, less than three feet, a putt that even a child can make. A voice in Alex's head says exactly those words, that a child could in fact make the putt, and suddenly Alex finds that his hands feel disconnected from his arms, disconnected from feeling the grip. He stares at the cup, re-measures the distance with his Mind. He can feel the eyes of the spectators around him, feels uncomfortable with his stance, but he hits it anyway.

The ball rolls past the cup without even a thought of dropping in...rolls beyond to a three-foot distance. An anguished groan spills from the crowd and seeps into the deeper regions of Alex's brain. In his peripheral vision he sees his opponent shift his posture as he enters unexpectedly into a tie and entertains the prospect of winning a playoff. Alex tries to put the image out of his head, stands over his three-footer. Again he feels the disconnection, the numbness, an eerie tightness in his muscles. Three feet seems to stretch away into infinity. He knows that ordinarily he could make this putt fifty times over, but somehow he is not feeling himself, has lost his sense of Self.

His putter strikes the ball and the line is true, but the ball hesitates on the lip, seeming to defy gravity, and it hangs there. The tournament is over. Alex has lost. His opponent, who did little to win in the final moments, offers some words of consolation. The gallery has coalesced into a murmuring background, but Alex is not aware of any of it. He is lost in disappointment, asking himself, " How can this happen? Why did this happen to me?"

# "5 9"

As I approached my 60th birthday, I could not help but become enamored with the number 59. What was so great about the number 59? Well, though perilously close, it was not quite the dreaded 60. So each time I woke up in the morning during that year, I was still only 59 years old. I hung on to 59 like it was my youth, though obviously it was not. Also, my favorite number has a nice ring to it and a good rhythm, practically rolling off the tongue.

59 is a magic number in golf, and it became so in 1977. At the Memphis Classic at the Colonial Country Club, an official PGA event, on a 6500 yard plus par 72 course, Al Geiberger shot a 29 on the front nine, then turned around a shot a 30 on the back....59!!!

My Mind stumbles when I consider how a round like Geiberger's might unfold, starting with a perfect drive, then a fairway shot close to the pin, and finally a challenging putt that drains like water. And then this degree of performance follows again on the next hole, and then the next, and the next. To make the feat even more remarkable, Geiberger played in 102 degree heat on a very tough 7200 yard course.

Then, in 1991, Chip Beck shot a 30 on the front nine of the Sunrise Golf Club and a 29 on the back to score a 59 in the Las Vegas Invitational. In 1999 David Duval did it the hard way by shooting a 31 on the front at the PGA West Palmer Course and then a stunning 28 on the back to score an official 59 in the Bob Hope Chrysler Classic. Paul Goydos shot the same scores in the John Deere Classic in 2010 at the TPC Deere Run, which is a par 71. Geiberger, Beck, and Duval all scored theirs on a par 72 course. Also in 2010 Stuart Appleby shot a 59 in the Greenbrier Classic on the Old White Course, which is a par 70.

Not to be outdone, Annika Sorenstam shot a 59 on the LPGA tour in 2001, the only woman to have ever recorded such a miraculous score.

ANNIKA SORENSTAM and AL GEIBERGER

And that rounds up the very short list for mind-boggling scores of 59 on courses of 6500 yards or more during a PGA tour event. These few players are the high priests of low scores. When I ponder the expertise, concentration, emotional control, and athletic prowess that generated these scores, I am awestruck.

But a score of 59 causes one to stop and wonder. How does a golfer reach this seemingly unattainable summit? Could it be the clubs, the course, the golfer's rigorous discipline, or the countless hours of dedication on the practice range?

Or is it that the golfer experienced a synchronicity of Mind and body so finely tuned that he actually, for an extended period of time, experienced his true and Present Self?

If that is the case, what exactly is a true and Present Self, and how does this amazing state of being come about on the golf course?

# THE SELF

In essence, the golfer stands alone. There are no pitchers, catchers, or fielders as in baseball, or a defensive line or guards and centers that may be substituted at any time. There are no forwards as in soccer, no teammates working as a whole as in the sport of hockey. There are no substitutions. The competitive golfer stands alone, and therefore must rely on a cohesive sense of Self and a healthy valuation of his "I" -ness. He must rely on the core perception of how he experiences himself as a person.

He has only himself to rely on, or more accurately, his *Self*. So what is this Self that the competitor must rely on? When we look for it, we see that it is difficult to find.

For instance, your Self is not your body. You can see your body and measure it and take photos of it. It looks like you, acts like you, and is your ambassador into the world, but it is not your Self.

The Self is also not your brain. Yes, your brain is probably the greatest miracle of all, but it is the organic machine that houses and enables your Mind.

Your Mind is not your Self either, though it is definitely a contributor to your entire person.

The Self is illusive.

The Self has no color, cannot be smelled or weighed, and is invisible. And yet, it is you and you are it. It is that sense of "I" -ness that permeates everything a golfer does, the core sense as to "Who I Am".

The Self is a combination of Mind and body, so only when the two are acting in concert do they form the ultimate expression of the Self. The farther the Mind is out of synch with your body, the more you are not your Self. Your conscious Mind must be Present to be synchronized with your body, to be in your body, because your body is always in the Present.

The Self is the uniting principle that underlies all of your experience. It is the combination of "your body, your Mind, and the resulting emotions" that make up the Self. It is the union of elements that make up your thoughts, feelings, emotions, and sensations. The Self is the central experience of all that is thought and felt, with the Self as the subject of these observations. How a golfer sees, feels, and interprets his relationship with the world forms the core experience of his own unique Self.

So as a golfer, what kind of conditions within an individual athlete determines the ultimate expression of the Self? What exactly is going on in the Mind and body of a golfer when he shoots a 59? How can we understand the workings of something like the Self that cannot be measured or even directly observed?

We can start with the Self's relationship with time.

# THE "NOW" CLOCK

Humans experience time in three ways. They experience the past, the Present, and the future. But in reality, there is only one embodied time, and that is the Present.

1. The future is an exercise of the imagination, based on information gathered from the past and Present.
2. The past is a collection of memories stored in your brain and accessed by your Mind, but is not something that still exists.
3. Only the Present exists, and is happening even as you read this sentence.

When I was a little boy, my grandfather had a very ornate clock that he kept on his mantelpiece. It was about ten inches high and was covered with intricately stamped pieces of metal and had an elegant clock-face. To keep his precious clock safe, he kept it in a glass dome, thereby keeping the eroding influence of the outside world at bay.

The problem was, that during his move from an old house to a new house, the clock had been removed from the bell jar, packed, and shipped. In the process the clock hands broke off and were never found. So in its new home the clock sat timelessly on the mantelpiece, its face forever declaring that the only time within that glass dome was *Now.*

I loved the "Now Clock", as I called it, because although it never told me the time of day, it did make me think about time and how we perceive it.

My grandfather, who had a quirky sense of humor, added another detail to the whole mantelpiece clock enigma. Underneath the protective dome, he placed an extremely ancient copy of the H.G. Wells classic, "The Time Machine".

# THE TIME MACHINE

When H.G. Wells wrote his time travel novella in 1895, he was heralded as a visionary. A fanciful idea for its time, the concept of a machine that could take a human passenger through time, backwards or forwards, eventually became mainstream. Books, motion pictures, TV shows, comics, and even scientific speculation latched on to this idea until it became a fixture in our society. However, no matter how many great Minds have addressed the idea, including scientists like Einstein, one fact still remains. The human body is stuck in the Present. STUCK !!!! The body cannot travel a millisecond into the future or the past, no matter what you do to it. It remains in the Present night and day, and that's the way it's going to stay.

However, the Mind, with its seemingly infinite capabilities, does in fact have the ability to Time Travel, or so it seems. Often I find my Mind wandering back to the days of my childhood or rocketing forth to next summer's golf outings with my friends. Or the Time Traveling Mind might take shorter trips, like "Where did I put my glasses?" or, "I wonder if it is going to rain," or "What are we going to do for dinner?"

On the golf course, things get more complicated. "What if I hit it in the trap?" or "Will I blow *this* putt, too?" These are not questions you would ask yourself if you are firmly in the Present. These questions represent trips back-and-forth in time, the Mind active or overactive, but certainly not in the Present. Your Mind cannot possibly be embedded and connected to your body if the Mind is Time Traveling.

# THE "NOW" WATCH

Again, we cannot attach some kind of brilliant machine to our Minds to measure and record these expeditions into the past and the future, big or small, because even though they seem as real as can be, they are not. They are constructs of the human Mind.

I know a female athlete who has a wonderful piece of jewelry not unlike my grandfather's clock. It is a watch that has a blank face with the word "NOW" printed on it. Whenever she finds her Mind in the process of Time Traveling, worrying about the unforeseeable future or dwelling in dark corners of the past, she feels unsettled and Anxious. She becomes de-regulated, having lost the regulation of her Self.

This tendency to Time Travel not only can lower the quality of her life, but can affect her athletic performance as well. However, she can simply look at her NOW watch and return to the Present and thereby return to being re-centered in her body to re-synchronize as her Self. By doing so she instantly feels better, more settled and focused on the Present reality around her instead of her imaginary future or emotionally charged past. By glancing at her NOW watch and ceasing to mentally Time Travel, she re-enters her body in the Present...she re-regulates.

# THE DOME

When I think about a professional golfer shooting a 59, I can picture him, through his amazing concentration and ability to Self-regulate, as being in an imaginary dome of intense focus, shutting out the outside world and its eroding influences. I picture in my Mind a larger version of the dome that protected my grandfather's timeless clock. Inside the dome there is only the Present, so the golfer performs as a *Now Golfer* with total *Presence.* Outside the dome are the possibilities of the future and the memories of the past. Outside the dome are Tension and Anxiety, the pressure of Expectations and the intensity of competition.

Just like the world inside the bell jar, the world inside the golfer's dome of focus should be a timeless world, a world of Now.

Preston likes to call this world inside of the protective dome the "Little Picture."

Outside the dome is "The Big Picture", which is the world that encompasses all of the magnets that pull us away from maintaining the Self's supreme focus.

In order to understand both the Little Picture and the Big Picture, the game of golf needs to be defined in its essence.

# GOLF DEFINED AND REDEFINED

---
*Golf is the Repetition of a
Single Movement in Time*

---

When we try to define golf, there are many angles to take, from whimsical definitions like Mark Twain's "a good walk spoiled", or "the word FLOG spelled backwards", or simply "the longest distance between two putts." An encyclopedia or dictionary definition would state that golf is "a game in which a small hard ball is propelled with various clubs into a series of widely spaced holes…"

For our purposes though, we would like to delve deeper, to explore the very essence of the game. Past champions have often summed up this essence in amazingly simple terms, like Harry Vardon's definition: "Hit it, find it, hit it again till it goes in the hole."

My favorite definition of golf is "a man standing in a field swinging a stick."

I like the following definition because of its simplicity and basic truth.

---
*To Golf is to Swing*

---

There is, in fact, precisely only one thing a golfer can do on the course, and that is to take a swing, and in order to take that swing, he can make only one movement. Whether the golfer is driving, chipping, duffing, or putting, he can do so with only one movement.

---

*A Golfer Can Only Make One Movement*

---

So golf is not the act of making a birdie, missing a putt, landing in the sand, or posting a record high or low score. It is not the act of competition. It is not winning or losing.

In its essence:

---

*Golf is the repetition of a Single Movement in Time*

---

The mention of *time* in our refined definition of golf is of utmost importance, because we have seen that as golfers we are all Time Travelers of sorts. Our Minds, as disciplined as they may or may not be, are drawn constantly and magnetically into the past and future. To make our *Single Movement in Time*, we must be firmly anchored in the Present, here, *Now*, in the moment.

So if golf is a *Single Movement in Time,* the time we are referring to is the Present. And though the real time is actually always *Now*, the Present can be a frustratingly hard thing to find. For instance, if you were to choose a target, like the pin, or the center of the fairway, or the cup, you are actually choosing a target in the future... a target that you are *intending* to hit.

If you are keeping a target in Mind, your Mind has Time Traveled into the future and you are no longer in the Present where your body permanently resides, and are therefore out of sync and not your ultimate Self.

When a golfer is in the Little Picture, he is firmly in the Present with no Time Traveling into the past and no ventures into the Future. The golfer enjoys a cohesive sense of Self and a strong and resilient Self-valuation. His Mind and body are dedicated to the essence of the game of golf, performing a *Single Movement in Time.*

A round of golf is simply a linear succession of segmented instances of *Single Movements in Time.* To play his best, a golfer must immerse his Mind/body solely within each separate segment of time. The flow of swings disconnects and reconnects with each successive shot in single separate segments of time.

For instance, in a par 72 score, there are 72 individual segments of time. Within each of those isolated segments is a *Single Movement in Time*, disconnected from the one before it and the one after it...each shot within the Little Picture.

---

*Within the Little Picture resides the simple and elegant geometry of the perfect golf movement*

---

The Big Picture, conversely, is everything happening outside the dome, the various time magnets and concentration magnets that seek to undermine the purity of a *Single Movement in Time.*

# THE BIG PICTURE

There are a variety of Time Travel magnets to pull the *Mind* away from the Present and to stop the *Mind* from communicating efficiently with the body.

The "Big Picture" is the greatest offender. It embodies a thought process that entices, mesmerizes, and seduces the *Mind* into traveling out of the moment and into the future. When on or off the golf course, the average person spends a great deal of his or her time in the Big Picture, for the imagined future of the world resides there.

Unfortunately, on the golf course, the Big Picture is the slayer of success.

The Big Picture can also be viewed as the admiration of the Self by the Self and the accompanying desire to be admired by others.

For example, let's imagine a child of twelve, proficient at golf, perhaps a prodigy, who looks forward to the possibilities that unfold before her as she matures. She lives in a very competitive world, so it is natural for her to compare herself to others. She looks at her classmates, her fellow golfers, the older like-minded athletes in her region, and her idols and inspirations…and she measures herself. She measures herself by the Expectations of her parents and her family, by her peers, and by the predispositions of her culture. From these internal measurements of Expectation and desire spring fantasies of what *may come to pass* in an imagined future.

In this imagined future there are tournaments won, victories gained through last minute brilliance that leave crowds gasping. Her parents are thrilled and proud and shower adulation on her like confetti in a parade. She wins the admiration of her schoolmates, her fellow golfers, and the public. Later, as the television cameras focus on her brilliance, she captures the attention and hearts of the public at large. She wins important tournaments, is heralded for her hard work and determination, praised for her character and good looks, envied for her seemingly endless charisma. Her face adorns the covers of magazines, flashes constantly on the television, is recognized and adored throughout the world. She signs autographs, travels to exotic places, drives expensive cars, wears chic outfits, buys elegant jewelry, meets the love of her life and marries in the wedding of the century, moves into a giant custom made mansion, raises children by the pool. Her many major victories become legend while her place in golf history remains unparalleled.

These are the types of fantasies the aspiring golfing Mind can produce, and without exception, they all occur in the future.

The Big Picture is always in the future, and when it is happening in the Mind, the Mind is not in the Present, is not communicating with the body, and cannot possibly produce a good golf shot.

The Big Picture is a powerful Time Travel magnet.

---

*The Big Picture is the Killer of the Good Golf Swing*

---

The Big Picture rears its ugly head for the recreational golfer as well. Imagine that you are playing with your boss on a weekend getaway. You know that you qualify for that upcoming promotion, but your fellow employee and rival Fred Carney is also eligible and you never liked him anyway

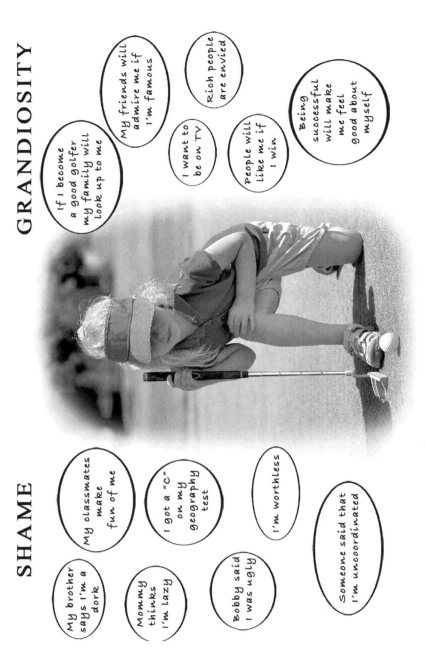

# GRANDIOSITY

If I become a good golfer my family will look up to me

My friends will admire me if I'm famous

Rich people are envied

I want to be on TV

People will like me if I win

Being successful will make me feel good about myself

# SHAME

My classmates make fun of me

I got a "C" on my geography test

I'm worthless

My brother says I'm a dork

Mommy thinks I'm lazy

Bobby said I was ugly

Someone said that I'm uncoordinated

## OUR INTERNAL DIALOG STARTS WHEN WE ARE YOUNG

and you are definitely more qualified. If you can just play bogey golf or better for the day, the boss can see what a consistent and reliable employee you are and give you the promotion instead of Carney...some time in the future.

Of course, since your Mind is in the future, perusing the infinite possibilities of the Big Picture, you can't hit a shot to save your life. You were going to discuss the promotion with your boss on 14, but since you spent so much time in the woods because you weren't in the Now for your *Single Movement in Time*, you failed to broach the subject. Later you discover that Carney got the promotion anyway, which is not surprising, because you made such an ass of yourself when you threw your pitching wedge into the lake on the final hole.

Or it can be simpler still. You might think, "Susie will be impressed if I blast this drive." And of course you won't blast it, because you are thinking about how impressed Susie *will be* and how your drive *will be*, and you are not in the Present and can't play golf worth a damn. Susie fails to be impressed when your drive veers impossibly to the right and shatters the windshield of a passing car. This is the evil dilemma of the Big Picture.

Surprisingly, the Big Picture does play an important part in the development of a good golfer or any good athlete for that matter. It is the *motivation* that provides the juice that fuels the engine of success. In order to become the best you can be at anything, one must have the *desire* to succeed in that endeavor, and the Big Picture embodies the desire to be admired by the *Self* and by others. By using this desire as fuel one can dedicate oneself to the endless hours on the practice range, the putting greens, and the throes of competition to reap the rewards promised by the fulfillment of these desires. So even though ultimately the Big Picture is the destroyer of all good golf swings, it is initially helpful in the formation of the good golf swing by providing a reason to work hard.

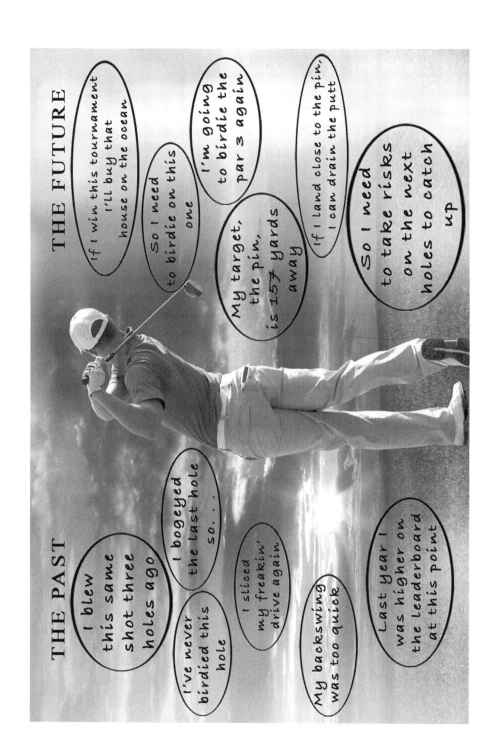

The Big Picture also comprises most of the world we live in. When not concentrating on an exacting task, one can live in the Big Picture without too many harmful effects. Just like anything else, elements of the Big Picture like Anxiety and Tension can be dangerous to one's health when present in large doses. However, Anxiety and Tension can also cause runners to run faster, creative people to be more creative, and dissatisfied people to seek satisfaction. Many people in sports, theater, art, and business are plagued with Anxiety and yet are able to use this unpredictable energy to their benefit. Golf, however, is one of those exceptions where Anxiety and the resulting muscular Tension never produce a good outcome.

There is also a sense of "absoluteness" in the Big Picture. We interpret the world of the future as something that will be safe for us, that tomorrow will be alright, that we will not die of a heart attack during the night, that nuclear war will not break out at lunchtime, that the doctor will not give us two weeks to live, and that we will not be struck by lightning on the eighth tee. Within this perception of absolutism is the concept that a person can trust his body to perform in a trusted way that gives one a sense of safety. This same trust allows us to drive and walk and perform everyday tasks without interference from the Mind. This implicit trust is key to our sense of existing comfortably within the world.

Since the Big Picture comprises most of the world we live in, we need to embrace it and understand it, but we must not let it interfere with our golf swing.

# THE LITTLE PICTURE

The Little Picture is comprised of what exists in the Present, in the Now. In golf, the Little Picture is the seamless execution of a Single Movement in Time. That means no Time Traveling...no jumping into an imagined and Grandiose future, no drifting into the past. Period. Just one movement in the Present that your body has been repeatedly trained to do in the Now through hard work, discipline, and an extremely dedicated practice routine. It is a work of Trust.

And so the golf swing evolves, different for everyone, but stored within the muscle memory of the athlete, imbedded in the Mind's Implicit Procedural Memory System...the same memory system that allows us to confidently walk and run and drive a car. The Little Picture is A *Single Movement in Time* refined down to just the golf swing itself, a smooth flowing motion that is graceful and purposeful and elegant.

The only way a human body can function at its optimum athletic capacity is for the Right Brain and the body to unite, or *synchronize*. These synchronizations create the finest of athletic achievements. To be in the Now for this marvel of athletics, the Left Brain must remain quiet and the Right Brain must be unhindered and unbothered to do its job. There can be no *Swing Thoughts*, for they are incarnations of the Left Brain. There can be no picturing of a target on the course, like the green or a safe landing spot, for that target would lie in the future and would take the

Mind out of the body. There can be no thoughts of disaster or success, for they too would lie in the future, and once again, the Mind would be out of the body. Even the thought of contacting the ball is in the future, because the player has not actually done it yet, so once again the Mind could be magnetized out of the body. The Right Brain must be without mental distractions to achieve full focus, and the focus of the Right Brain is the making of the *Single Movement in Time.* Making the *Single Movement in Time* again and again on the golf course is what leads to the ultimate relationship between the golfer and the ball and the lowest score possible on that particular day.

The golfer's body, to be in the Little Picture, must be free of muscular Tension and Anxiety. A golfer cannot be Tense or Anxious and still hit a perfect stroke. Picture the golfer within the giant bell jar. Inside this enormous glass dome the golfer performs a golf swing unhindered by the outside world, a Single Movement in Time.

Outside the glass dome exist all the aspects of the Big Picture, the time magnets of past failure and future Grandiosity, the Expectations of success or failure, the expected path of the ball, the ball itself, the outcome of the swing, the mental instructions that helped train the swing, the actual golf score, the intended golf score, situational pressures like a match or tournament, the varying emotional stressors that your friends and relatives bring to bear. Outside the dome the chaos and irrational perfection of the world collide to form what the Buddhists call *Samsara,* the intricate machinations of the world in all their disturbing complexities. Inside the glass is a slice of heaven on a human scale, the perfection of a single athletic motion, the *Single Movement in Time,* the Little Picture.

Total Focus

The
Past

The
Future

The
Present

What if the golfer was protected from the desire of winning or the fear and anguish of losing? What if there was no outcome to the shots, but just the joy of swinging, free from Anxiety, a man standing in a field making a motion? Only then would the golfer make a *Single Movement in Time*, a repeatable swing.

However, outside the dome, the golfer is subjected to the elements, to the pressure of Expectations, the fear of failure, the involuntary tightening of the muscles, the wandering of concentration, the loss of tempo, the suppressed storm of emotions brewing inside.

This is the world a golfer must live in. He is subjected to every distraction and deterrent in the game, and yet he performs just as though he were in the giant protective dome. He continually makes a *Single Movement in Time* undeterred by the powerful world around him.

He operates in a dome of concentration where he golfs in the Present, a *Now Golfer*, in the Little Picture...reaching his potential as his true Self.

# YOU MUST BE PRESENT TO WIN

Speaking of winning, although a 59 is an incredible score, it is not a tournament won, but one fourth of a tournament won. It is truly an amazing feat to shoot such a low score, but to consistently shoot under par golf for four days is another thing entirely. Sometimes, in the heat of the closing moments of a tightly contended golf tournament, a 72 is what is needed to take home the gold. And even more pressurized is the tournament won or lost in a sudden death play-off after a tie on the final hole.

There have been some amazing rounds of brilliance strung together back-to-back, enough to win a tournament and enter the record books. Ernie Els, the 2003 Mercedes Champion, shot his 72 holes in a remarkable 31 under par. At the Bob Hope classic in 2009, Steve Stricker shot 33 under par on 72 holes of what is a 90 hole tournament.

To emphasize the pressure and difficulty of professional golf, it should be noted that Steve Stricker did not win that tournament in his fifth round, but was overtaken by Tony Perez.

And to turn it up a notch once again, these tournaments were not majors. How about the pressure of sudden death in a Major Championship? What about the incredible stress of being on the brink of winning your first Major going into the final holes with finest golfers in the world breathing down your neck? The record under par score for 72 holes in a Major Championship is held by Tiger Woods, who carded a 19 under par performance to capture the 2000

British Open. It was a day when Tiger was definitely feeling himself. Tiger trusted his body implicitly, knowing that he had trained his swing to unfold in the Present. Observing this, he would say, " I try to never let my mind interfere with what my body is trying to do."

# THE LANDSCAPE OF THE MIND

*"The great pleasure and feeling in my right brain is more than my left brain can find words to tell you..."* Dr. Roger Sperry, upon accepting the Nobel Prize for his split-brain research.

The psychological and physiological differences between the right and left hemisphere of the human brain were discovered in 1981 by Dr. Roger Sperry, for which he won a Nobel Prize. We have no doubt heard the terms before, but exactly what do they mean and how do they affect our play on the golf course?

The left hemisphere of the brain is responsible for such functions as problem solving, reasoning, critical thinking, language, math and science. Here resides our short-term memory and our ability to manipulate numbers and measurements. The Left Brain likes to look at the world in parts or segments. People who are Left Brain dominant tend to be accountants, engineers, librarians, computer programmers, and bankers.

The right hemisphere produces our subjective thoughts, our creativity and intuition. Importantly for us as golfers, the right hemisphere harbors our feelings and ability to feel, as well as our long-term memories. The Right Brain communicates directly with the body, allowing the Mind to *feel* the body in motion.

*The Right Brain communicates directly with the body,*
*allowing the Mind to feel the body in motion.*

The right side of the brain is a good place to visit when you want to create a feeling that you will never forget...like a perfect golf swing, for instance!

The right side of the brain is also responsible for perceiving actions or concepts as a whole, rather than a segmented conglomeration. People who are right side dominant tend to be writers, artists, psychoanalysts, recreational directors, interior designers, and...professional athletes. These right side dominant folks like to be outdoors and interact with nature while doing athletic activities. What a perfect match for the golf course!

Golf is a game of quantification and assessment as well as feel. It is a game of geometry and physics, a game of measurements and estimates, of objective awareness and critical thinking. It is a game of sequences. A great golfer should maintain a balance between these two equally essential parts of the brain.

What is crucial to understand, and what is crucial in order to maximize a golfer's potential and performance... is to know when to be in the left side of the brain and when to be in the right side... so it is crucial for the golfer to know when to Transition from the Left Brain to the Right Brain and then back again to the Left Brain.

After all, golf is a game of Transitions. A golfer makes Transitions from the real world to the golf course, from one golf course to another, from one hole to another, from one shot to another, from one club to another, from the Practice Swing to the actual swing.

# Left Brain Hemisphere

# Right Brain Hemisphere

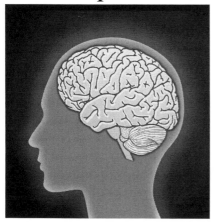
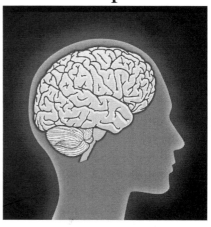

Measurements
Calculations
Language
Critical Thinking
Science
Problem Solving
Short Term Memory

Subjectivity
Creativity
Intuition
Spatial Cognition
Mapping
Ability to Feel
Long Term Memory
Athleticism

The Transition from the Left Brain to the Right Brain is essential before beginning our *Single Movement in Time.* For instance, when a player steps onto the tee, the Left Brain is busy at work as the player considers the myriad conditions of the hole as it stretches out before him.

When a golfer is assessing his shot, he must estimate the distance to his target or the hole as accurately as possible. The left side of the brain loves to solve problems, so by figuring out a strategy to reach the hole in fewest strokes possible, the Left Brain is in its glory. The golfer must also calculate the effect of the wind, the lie of the land, and his own capabilities.

He must then select the correct club from a very Left-Brained set of tools. Golf clubs are all about math and physics, about the degrees of loft and momentum of mass at the end of a variably flexible shaft. The player checks the distance from the markers, calculates changes due to pin placement and the direction and strength of the wind. These mental mathematics, the calculations and measurements and estimates are all primarily Left-Brained activities and are absolutely essential to good golfing.

In fact, the better you are at using your Left Brain, the more accurate your shots will have the potential to be. So now that all the math and physics have been settled and decisions have been made, it is time to make a Transition.

In order to execute our *Single Movement in Time* correctly, we need to Transition from the quantifying capabilities of the Left Brain to the sensate awareness and athleticism of the Right Brain. Having downloaded all the information gathered by the Left Brain, the Right Brain is ready to allow that information to Transition into a sensation of how the swing should feel. To truly be in the Little Picture where he can feel his body, the golfer must leave the Left Brain behind. To be totally in the Little Picture and execute our *Single Movement in Time*, we must have the awareness of feeling our swing unfolding in the manner it has been repeatedly trained to do.

---

*You Cannot Feel the Body Without the Mind*

---

And what exactly does *feeling* mean?

---

*Feeling is the Conscious Awareness of the Sensation of Movement Within the Body*

---

You cannot feel the body without the Mind, and you feel it best when it is unhindered by cognitive thought. Feeling or "feel" is the conscious awareness of the sensation of body movement. The Mind *knows* the body through feeling. It is how they communicate.

---

*The Mind Feels the Body*

---

When the Mind is Present in the body, as it is when the Right Brain is active, the golfer can have a "felt sense" of the shot. That way the Mind tracks movement of the body, never getting ahead or behind of the swing as it unfolds. The more the Mind is in the Left Brain, the more it loses touch with the sensation of a moving awareness or feel of the shot. There is too much background chatter. So there must be a Transition from the cognitive Left Brain to the sensate awareness of the Right Brain before you can truly feel the unfolding of a good golf shot.

The more imbedded the Mind is in the body, the more the Mind is in the Present, the more the Mind can *feel* the body. When the Mind is Present, the Mind is capable of collecting the most information about movement through *feeling.* When the Mind is embedded in the body, the maximum amount of information is available, giving the golfer a sense of moving awareness. That way the golfer has a *felt* sense of the swing. In the Present moment, the Mind and body are blissfully joined. Then, when the swing happens, it is a joyous union of what we think and what we feel. It is happening right Now, a *Single Movement in Time.* This great *feeling* upon hitting a good shot, this bio-feedback of rightness, rolls through the body like a revelation.

Golf is a game of the senses. No other game incorporates so many feelings. It is a game you play within yourself, unique in its isolation and investigation into one's Self. When asked what he liked about golf, Harvey Firestone answered:

---

*"I like the way it feels."*

---

There is a sensuality to hitting a great shot. An unknown player once said:

---

*"Golf is the most erotic of games."*

---

# THE TWO GIFTS

It is no secret that golf is an unforgiving game. The rules are strict and lacking in generosity.

And yet, there are two gifts in golf, and they often go unused or are simply misunderstood. These two gifts are:

1. The *Practice Swing*.
2. The ability to *Step Away From The Ball*.

# THE GRAND REHEARSAL

---

*From the Rules of Golf...A practice swing is not a practice stroke and may be taken at any place, provided the player does not breach the Rules.*

---

If we were to take practice *strokes*, or Mulligans, during play, there would undoubtedly be violence on the golf course from the resulting snail like pace. The Practice Swing, however, is considered to be both timely and within the rules of etiquette. If properly used, the Practice Swing can reduce Time Traveling and other mental distractions from the Big Picture and help anchor the golfer in the Present so that the stroke itself can be felt and maximized.

The Practice Swing is the best tool a golfer can use to craft a good golf shot. The Practice Swing is the "Grand Rehearsal". It is all about the feel of *the Single Movement in Time*, about the feel of the swing in motion. The Practice Swing is a Transitional Mind mechanism for going from the Left Brain to the Right Brain.

Many players use the Practice Swing as a loosening up swing, or a *Tension Relieving Swing*, so that the body will be relaxed and fluid during the actual stroke itself. There is a lot to be said for a Tension relieving swing, but it should not be mistaken for a Practice Swing nor used in its place.

Sometimes the actual movement of the pre-shot routine will calm the player down, just getting them back into their bodies, like the results of a ritual. This might work two or three times, but in the long run will drop away because the cause of Tension has not been addressed.

Do not think the Tension relieving swing is a substitute for the Practice Swing. To do so would be giving up one of your two rare and precious gifts.

If one is not satisfied with the first Practice Swing, however, it would be wise to re-orient, and through *feel* find the Practice Swing that best fits the upcoming shot. It is here that one must settle into a comfort zone where the Practice Swing is used to its fullest without the golfer feeling peer pressure from overuse and thereby delaying the rhythm of the game.

If a golfer feels rushed during the Practice Swing, if he feels eyes on his back, if he feels the pressure of real or perceived disapproval from those who wait, the actual stroke will be rushed and out of rhythm. The golfer must see this time as his own and use it as he feels fit, and rightly so, for it is a gift that has been given by a strict book of rules that is just not known for gifting.

Once comfortable with this golfing gift and the notion that the time allotted is the time you deserve, the Practice Swing is to be executed with certain goals in Mind.

# GIFT #1 – THE PRACTICE SWING

Stepping up to the tee, the player's Left Brain swings into gear. The player assesses the drive and holds the appropriate club in his hands. He observes the wind, its speed, its direction, its possible and likely effect on the flight of the ball. He scans the outlay of the land, the topography, the safe landing spots, the possible pitfalls. He calls on his experience, remembering how he has faired in the past with this particular club under similar conditions. The golfer considers odds, computes likelihoods, determines strategy. All of this information is initiated and evaluated in his Left Brain. He determines his shot. He takes his stance and downloads all this information into his body so that he can *feel* the results of his calculations in his Practice Swing.

The activity of the Left Brain must now *Transition* to activity of the Right Brain in order for the player to *feel* the shot.

The Transition from the Left Brain to the Right Brain occurs during the Practice Swing, so that the body can become accustomed to the tremendous amount of information it has just downloaded and make any necessary adjustments to the *feel* of the swing.

The Practice Swing is the vessel in which that Transition takes place.

So the player:

1. Collects vital information.
2. Decides the shot based on that information.

3. Transitions from Left-Brained thinking information to Right-Brained feeling sensations and spatial perceptions through use of the Practice Swing.

What a gift!

The player now has a preview of the way the *Self* feels in the actual swing.

The Practice Swing has many benefits:
1. It allows the Left Brain to Transition away from "swing thoughts" to the feel of the muscles flowing as they are trained to do.
2. Takes the Mind from outside the body and imbeds it inside the body.
3. Acts as an emotional regulator.
4. Helps keep the golfer in the Little Picture.

# GIFT #2 - STEPPING AWAY FROM THE BALL

When watching a golfer approach the ball and settle over it, getting ready to swing, one can often judge the player's state of Mind by his body language. It is very common to see a waggle or two, a lifting and releasing of the shoulders, a minor change in footing and body position. An observer may also discern Tension or Anxiety storing itself within the body. The player's Mind may not be in his body, bouncing back and forth from the possibilities of the future to the victories and failures of the past, then back again to the future. If the player's Mind is not rooted in the Now, if there is no Presence, then the Mind and body cannot possibly synchronize to make a *Single Movement in Time* correctly.

A golfer can, of course, sense this discrepancy within himself and within his Self all too well. The muscles Tense, the breath is shallow, and any sense of fluidity vacates the athlete's frame. The player has become off balance, having lost the *Presence* of Mind/body synchronization. Many players, when sensing this discomfort, this unhappiness with the body, will just go ahead and hit the ball anyway. This is what Stewart Cink refers to as an *Anyway Shot,* as in: " I really don't feel comfortable or confident hitting this shot, but I'm going to hit it *anyway.*"

Show me a golfer who has never hit an *Anyway Shot*. That golfer does not exist. The entire purpose of the *Anyway*

*Shot* is to just get the darned thing over with so the player will no longer feel the present discomfort and will hopefully and magically regain the use of his body and Mind and hit a good shot. However, the *Anyway Shot* almost always turns out to be a bad shot. Now the previous bad situation has been compounded and the following shot becomes an even worse situation with even more lack of presence and more pressure to hit it "anyway."

The solution for this situation is Gift #2... Stepping Away from the Ball.

If the shot does not feel right, if the Mind is not in the body, if the body feels Tense, if you are about to hit the freaking thing anyway...Step Away From the Ball.

This will give you a chance to re-synchronize, to find your wandering Mind and put it back in your body where it belongs, to unwind your muscular Tension, and to escape the certainty of worsening your score and your resulting mental, emotional, and physical state by hitting an *Anyway Shot*.

Step Away From the Ball. Get back into your body. Turn off the Time Machine. Find your Self in the Present moment. Breathe. Return to your shot.

Take another Practice Swing to feel the shot and enact the right hemisphere of the brain. This allows the golfer to preview a regulated sense of Self for that shot. Make a *Single Movement in Time*. Enjoy the beauty of the motion. As the ball leaves the club you too will become a spectator at that point. Observe the fruits of your labor and the joy of the ability to make the Single Movement. Yes, feel the joy of it. That's why you ventured out onto the golf course in the first place.

Many pros will not Step Away From the Ball because they see it as a sign of weakness. They are afraid that other players will watch their aborted attempt and judge them as inferior or lacking in mental toughness. The reality is, there is no weakness in Stepping Away from the Ball but simply the desire to do one's best under pressure. Hitting an *Anyway Shot* is a sign of weakness, and a guarantee of a bad score and a miserable round emotionally and mentally. Use your gifts. Take a Practice Swing. Take a few if you have to. If you don't feel the Presence of Mind/body synchronization, Step Away From the Ball. Allow the feeling of Tension to dissipate, then return to your Practice Swing. Download all the information from the Left Brain into the Right Brain so it can be changed into the appropriate awareness of feeling that approximates the best shot. Take another Practice Swing because the information in the last Practice Swing has long since left the building and is unavailable. Feel the Practice Swing. Feel the freedom of the "man in the field" gracefully and rhythmically swinging the stick, with no intended outcome other than the beauty of the movement itself. Then you can get back into the Little Picture and enjoy the unfolding of your *Single Movement in Time*. Feel the Presence of your regulated Self within the shot, enjoy the moment, and play the best golf that you are capable of playing. Used correctly, the Practice Swing is the Now Golfer's best friend.

# SWING THOUGHTS

The practice range is, of course, not just some infuriating exercise designed to instill madness into the most stable of personalities. It is an indispensable tool in the development of a finely tuned golf swing. The practice range is where our strokes evolve from their infancy, where our Minds and bodies learn what is one of the most demanding and unforgiving of motions. Through practice the muscles are trained, the timing of the swing is honed, and the Mind learns to focus on the intricate series of contractions and releases that eventually become a single swing.

When we are learning these motions, we often are wise enough to seek advice from a qualified professional. From this person's experience we gain instructions that help us solve our individual swing problems and develop our swings to their maximum efficiency. However, there is a right way and a wrong way to bring this knowledge back to the practice range. It is a good idea to come away from your lesson with a single mental instruction, or Swing Thought. The best Swing Thought is the one that allows the player to "give himself over" to the natural unfolding of his golf movement, unfettered by cognitive thought. With such singular attention one can practice that single instruction on the driving range until it is incorporated into the swing in a positive way.

A typical instruction of this kind would be " Close the club face a little," or " Increase your shoulder turn." These instructions, over a period of years, make up the foundation of a good golf swing.

However, if you bring too many Swing Thoughts with you to the driving range, your brain, as willing as it may be, will fall into a state of confusion and overstimulation. Your body will be unable to decipher these myriad instructions and the result will be a de-regulated golfer.

Swing Thoughts can be to your benefit in very small doses, but in larger doses are the equivalent of a computer crash. A sage instructor was once heard to say, "Anyone who can play with all these Swing Thoughts in his head is simply not human!"

# Swing Thoughts

Pause at the top

Rotate the shoulders

Think about your target

Don't think about your target

Choose your target

Full follow through

Weight on front foot

Minimize knee flex

Keep the shoulders still

Make solid contact

Caress it

Break your wrists

Exagerate knee flex

Turn to the finish

Keep your head still

Proper balance

Pound it

Don't tense up

Don't break your wrists

Feet Parallel

Narrow your stance

No shoulder sway

Correct grip

Make an L with your rear elbow

Knees slightly bent

Stay on top of the ball

Let the club drop

Widen your stance

Don't drop the shoulder

Rotate back & thru

Relax

Watch the back of the ball

One piece start

Lengthen the backswing

Close your club face

Grip down for control

Swing slowly

Accelerate the club face

Weight on back foot

# THE FEARLESS UNFOLDING

The human body is a miracle of engineering. When hitting a golf ball, a golfer must coordinate no less than two hundred bones with the help of over six hundred muscles. These muscles are controlled by the brain, an organic computer consisting of over a hundred billion neurons. These neurons communicate with the one hundred trillion cells in your body. No dummies themselves, each cell contains the ability to store the same amount of information contained in five encyclopedias. In concert, these miracles of biological human life can somehow conspire to cleave an errant five iron into the woods or drain a seemingly impossible hole-in-one.

In real life, we develop an entitled attitude toward the mechanisms of body consciousness. Somehow we forget about the complex interactions of our physiology as we make our way through life.

Take Anne for example, housewife and mother, part-time realtor, and a dedicated amateur golfer. After practicing a few irons at the range, she is off to pick up her two kids from school in the mini-van. Once the kids are in the car, she makes her way through heavy traffic in route to the grocery store. Anne talks to a client on the cell phone as she checks her grocery list on the center console. Her son is acting up in the back seat, so she keeps an eye on him as well, speeding through daunting rush hour traffic at fifty miles per hour. She turns her head to give her son "the look", realizes she doesn't really need paper towels at the store and mentally crosses it off her list, all the while chatting away to her client. She takes a sip of coffee, dials a new number on the phone, and takes a left turn. The big question is, if Anne is involved in these many varied and demanding tasks...who could be driving the car?

The answer is that Anne was using skills that she had trained her Self to do so well that she no longer had to think about them...they simply happened automatically. The internal mechanism that allowed her to do this is what psychoanalysts call the Implicit Procedural Memory System, or IPMS. It is the internal mechanism that allows us to perform complex tasks without consciously instructing ourselves to do so.

The IPMS is the trained but unconscious side of the golf swing. At this level is the freewheeling non-cognitive letting go of the sequential unfolding of the learned golf swing. This is the level that we golfers hope to achieve, the unthinking natural "instinctual" part of the golf swing. It is this "instinctual" feeling that we all strive for. Any mental activity that interrupts the natural unfolding of this neuromuscular sequencing will throw it off.

It is this unfolding that we ultimately want to feel secure with. This is most difficult because during this unfolding is when we feel most Vulnerable because of the uncertainty of the outcome. We feel Vulnerable because we know that we must leave this unfolding alone in order to reach maximum potential. As human beings, we often have trouble just leaving things alone. This takes a tremendous amount of trust, trust in the body, trust in the Self, and trust in the learned motion of the golf swing. We feel like more of a witness to a process going on within us and outside of us at the same time. It is *inside* of us in that we are the "doers" and it is *outside* of us in that we are only conscious of its unfolding. It thereby feels like it is actually happening *to us* rather than us making something happen. Our cognitive and protective senses must not interfere. This "giving into" and "allowing" what we have trained ourselves to do is the secret of great golf movements.

Even as I type these words, my fingers automatically seek out and strike the correct keys without any Left-Brained instructions on my part. The neuromuscular system in my fingers learned these typing motions through repetition and then integrated them into my unconscious skills. I may be thinking with my Left Brain about the words and letters that I would like to type, but my fingers work without any coaching.

When I was a child, I learned to walk, falling down a lot in the process, but could eventually do it effortlessly without thinking. Later on I learned to ride a bike, but it took some training and some skinned knees. But through practice I learned and now I can ride without any internal instructions on how to balance and how to move my legs or even how to steer. There is uncertainty within the outcome of all these tasks, and with uncertainty comes the possible Vulnerability to outcome. But I don't worry about the downside of possible outcomes, am fearless about their unfolding, because I <u>trust</u> that my learned motions will overcome that uncertainty.

I trust this process so much, in fact, that I do not really worry about the results of these skills even though I have crashed my bike in the past and have certainly tripped and fallen down.

I still trust my unthinking motions. I still allow them to unfold fearlessly.

Pres provided some examples of the Left Brain interfering with co-ordination.

"Once one of my clients was complaining to me about the complexity of his putting swing, of all the gremlins contained therein from back swing to wobbly execution.

He was totally caught up in mechanics and was thinking about them during execution of the swing. These "Swing Thoughts" are the killers of a good golf movement, and I had to figure out a way for my client to drop the Swing Thoughts and trust the same internal process that allowed Anne to flawlessly drive her car. So I asked my client, who we will call Martin, to try an experiment on the way home from our session."

" Martin, when you drive home, I want you to concentrate on the mechanics of driving your car. I want you to notice how tightly you hold the steering wheel, how fast you turn it during a turn, how far you turn it, and if you have turned it too far or not enough for that particular turn. I would also like you to pay particular attention to the weight of your foot on the accelerator, the angle of the toes within your shoes, and the distance in inches between the accelerator and the brake. When you do use the brake, I want you to notice the pressure on the pedal, stay exactly two feet inside the center line and match the speed limit exactly. Do this exercise all the way home, and when you get there, please give me a call."

Well, I did get the call a short time later and Martin was agitated.

" You won't believe this Doc, but I almost wrecked my car on the way home. I got all caught up in the motion of my hands on the wheel, and my feet felt like a couple of numb clubs on the end of my ankles. I couldn't maintain a constant speed and my turns were jerky and inaccurate."

"Martin," I said, " the driving instructions were like Swing Thoughts. They occupied your Mind with the mechanics of driving, so that driving became a series of poorly executed commands. In fact, you are an excellent and skilled driver if you would simply let your IPMS do what it does, and not confuse it with commands."

"So I'm thinking too much about mechanics when I'm putting?"

"Exactly. You already know how to putt. It's just that you are letting Swing Thoughts interfere with your highly trained and competent motion. The idea is to keep the controlling part of the Mind out of the natural unfolding of the Implicit Procedural Memory process. Trust your *Self* to do the putting. You can *feel* what is right."

# "A GOOD WALK SPOILED"

"The driving experiment worked a little too well in that there was an element of danger in thinking 'driving thoughts' while trying to operate a motor vehicle," Pres continued. " I felt a little bit bad about that, so I wanted to do the same experiment in a safer way. So when the next client came in, named Martha, who was also complaining about her putting, I decided to use a different tactic."

" I want you to walk across the room for me Martha. "

Martha got up from her chair and walked effortlessly and gracefully across the room, pirouetted, and glided back.

"Okay. Now I want you to give yourself some walking instructions, some *Walking Thoughts*. Right leg forward, left hand back, then right hand back, left leg forward. Pay particular attention to the angle of the knee, the lift of the ankle, and the angle of the foot at contact. Also mentally measure the length of each stride on each side as well as the tightness in your shoulders and elbows. Look down at your feet, and then look where you are going. Alternate these processes. "

Martha again walked across the room, but she looked amazingly uncoordinated where only moments before she moved like a graceful dancer.

"Wow," she said, " I moved like a klutz."

"And you will putt like a klutz if you allow putting *Swing Thoughts* to dominate your innate coordination. Your trained neuromuscular system, the one that helps you walk so gracefully by moving in a way that feels natural, wants to shine. You simply must allow her to do so. The trust in your trained movements that helps you to walk so gracefully will also help you to putt gracefully."

# PUTTING TO NOWHERE

---

*"Concerning swing and techniques, I don't know diddly squat. When I'm playing well, I don't even take aim".....*
*Freddy Couples*

---

Harry Vardon, one of the greatest putters who ever lived, but a putter who experienced difficulties later on in his career, discovered an amazing thing about his putting one afternoon when the sun began to set. The light faded and shadows grew long, but instead of noticing a resulting diminishment in his putting, Vardon noticed a surprising *improvement.* He intuited from his experience that the factor that had changed was his vision, his inability to clearly see the cup. His target, the cup, existed clearly as a target in his future and therefore caused the Mind/body relationship to lack synchronization. The lack of clear vision caused Vardon to rely on his sense of *feel* for his putts rather than his sense of *vision.*

The sense of vision and its target-oriented affiliation with the future hampered the genius of his Right Brain. The Right Brain does its job by its sense of *feel.* By feeling his putt, Vardon used the right hemisphere of his brain to unleash his most coordinated Self. To *see* his target drew him into the future and out of his body, but to *feel* his target allowed him to stay Present and synchronize with his body so that he could enjoy his *Single Movement in Time*. By losing his clear visual target, by "Putting to Nowhere", by *feeling* his way to the cup, Vardon became a better putter.

Harry Vardon

Swing thoughts can also cause problems during putting. Golf brain activity researcher Dr. Debbie Crews measured electrical frequencies in both hemispheres of the brain during the putting process. Golfers who concentrated on stroke mechanics exhibited intense brain patterns of poor synchronization, whereas a player who putted while only *feeling the putt* displayed calm and focused brain activity. With scientific evidence pointing to the destructive capabilities of Swing Thoughts during the putting process, one can only seek to banish these nagging instructions from the Mind. So it is not *how* you think that affects your putting, but how you are able to *not think.*

First of all, a golfer can't make a putt, he can only make a stroke. For practice, most golfers tend to bang out some big shots on the driving range, maybe make a few chips, and then hit the fairways. This practice behavior is a type of denial, since putting tends to make up about 42 – 50 percent of the shots that we hit, and that's when we are playing our best. The average golfer can expect to hit about half of his shots while on the green, so this aspect of the game obviously needs to be strong and consistent. Practice on the putting green, but practice in a way that reinforces the use of *Feel* through your Right Brain.

Some techniques that may help you practice.

1. Putt to *Nowhere* ...just make your putting stroke, without accompanying Swing Thoughts, and see where the ball ends up. Try not to compete with yourself over the outcome. Just make your Single Movement in Time, allowing your Right Brain to be in the Present. If you sense that you have mechanical problems that are making your swing inconsistent, then choose a Swing Thought that you think may be an appropriate fix and take a Practice Swing using your chosen Swing Thought. Then step up to the ball, drop the Swing Thought, and once again putt to nowhere. Continue to do this until you *feel* the stroke as you hit the ball and

no longer sense that you are stringing together mechanical steps.

2. Move ten feet from the hole. Without looking at the hole, sense its *presence* as you practice putt. Remember, looking at the hole is looking into the future, a Left- Brained activity that takes you out of your body. After continuous practice of hitting without looking, you will be able to *feel* what ten feet *feels* like rather than what it *looks* like.

3. Use a Practice Swing each time before hitting your putt. Try to recreate the sense of *feel* from the Practice Swing in the actual swing. Feel the similarity between the Practice Swing and the Single Movement in Time.

# PUTTING SWING THOUGHTS

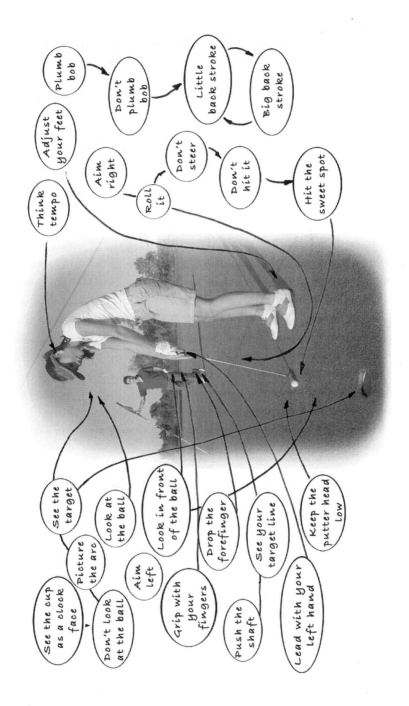

# KEEPING YOUR HEAD STILL

The most important motion to keep in mind while putting is not a motion at all, but in fact a lack of motion. To be a great putter, a Now putter, is to keep one's head still during the swing. That keeps the head and the eyes at the center of the swing and the rest of the body can move according to its Single Movement in Time.

More importantly, keeping the head still will prevent the eyes and head from moving toward the target...sneaking a peek at the cup...and into the future.

When I see a friend move his head during a putt, to sneak a peek, I like to kid him, "Oh, you probably thought the cup was going to move during your swing." Some players think that the only thing keeping the cup from moving is their willful stares as they look away from the ball (and ensure that they will miss). You cannot rivet the cup in place with your eyes, nor do you need to. Hopefully the cup will not move during the swing. The Practice Swing that you rehearsed before your putt is sufficient to assure you that you can *feel* the cup's location. The putter must trust his stroke, trust his body, trust his Practice Swing, and in the end, trust gravity when the ball falls into the cup.

It is our tendency as golfers, however, to look into the future. And that is exactly where the cup is in the perception of sinking a putt. As we have discovered, when looking into the future the Mind leaves the body and coordination suffers.

Therefore keeping the head still during the putt keeps your Self firmly rooted in the Now and able to *feel* the putt in the Present...therefore making the best putt possible.

KEEP YOUR HEAD STILL
*FEEL* THE PUTT IN THE PRESENT

After the ball has left your putter and is rolling toward the hole, then you can look up to watch the ball roll toward the cup and disappear into the hole because you have nothing to do with the outcome.

# LOOKING FORWARD

We are forward looking creatures. That is the way we are designed. Thousands of years ago, as man was evolving as a species, we were different from the other creatures around us. Unlike the eagle and the horse and the dolphin, our eyes are mounted in protective sockets on the front of our heads, instead of on the sides. As a result, our peripheral vision is only 140 degrees. We developed as a far-seeing species, constantly scanning the horizon for food, water, shelter, and the danger of predatory animals or rival tribes. We are really good at seeing and interpreting distant objects and landscapes. It is a skill that has served us well.

As golfers, this forward-looking tendency is both a good and a bad thing. Being able to gage distances certainly helps us choose the right club and estimate the logistics of our shots. But as we look into the distance, even a short distance (like a putt), we are looking into the future. In fact, anything we perceive in the distance, be it visual or conceptual, must by logic lie in the future. The future is unique. It is not a place we have visited yet. Ironically, whenever we *do reach* the perceived future, it turns out to be the Present. Just like in this sentence.

The human Body is always in the NOW. It remains in the Present at all times. The body has no Time Travel capabilities.

Only the Mind has the capacity to travel through time. When the Mind is traveling in the past or future, it cannot be in the Body since the Body is always in the Present, and as a result the Self is divided.

For example, Sandy, a top touring professional, stands on the 17th tee and addresses the ball. It is the final day of the tournament, and she is leading by one stroke. She possesses the dreaded and exciting knowledge that her competitors have signed their scorecards and wait in the clubhouse for an outcome they can no longer control. Her sister has flown in from Missouri just to watch the tournament, and watches anxiously in the gallery. Sandy's swing is a study in perfection, having been honed by the finest instruction and long hours on the course. She need only par this hole and the next one and the tournament is hers.

However... before Sandy begins her swing, her Mind begins to travel forward in time. She pictures herself clenching her fist in victory after birdying the 18th, the TV cameras swinging in close, her sister beaming from the gallery. There will be the victory interview, the presentation of the trophy (and the check), and a newfound momentum in her career that will carry her into the glorious spot reserved for her in the cherished history of Lady's Professional Golf. Her glowing face will adorn the covers of Golf Digest and Golf Magazine, and she will finally purchase that green Jaguar convertible she has always wanted.

Except for one thing... Sandy is just not herself at this moment in time. She is not her Self: the synchronized combination of her Mind and her body. She cannot be her Self because she is a person divided. Her body, permanently anchored in the Present, cannot perform its Single Movement in Time correctly because her Mind is not in her body. In the pressure of the moment, she hits the shot *anyway*, an *Anyway Shot*.

Sandy unleashes a smoking drive, loaded with spin and error, and the ball rockets to the right and over the crowd, bouncing from the trunk of a tree and into a deep sand trap. She looks over at her sister, who has always been hard on her, and watches a shadow of disappointment cross her face. Sandy then double-bogeys the hole and finishes in third place. Her spirits are crushed and the botched shot becomes etched into her memory like a scar that stays forever angry. She loses confidence in her abilities and misses the cut at the next tournament. The green Jaguar sits at the dealership, ownerless.

The future is no place to be when your body is trying to perform a precision task in the Present.

Or take Mike for example. As a talented top college player, he has struggled recently with his game, playing with streaks of brilliance that tend to terminate late in the match. On this particular day, he finds himself on 18, also up by a stroke. He has a 12 foot putt to win his match and once again become the number one player on his team. He steps up to the ball, knowing that his putting is his strength. However, his Mind begins to travel into the past through *remembering*, or backwards Time Traveling, and recalls a similar situation only a month prior. He had been playing a team match against a rival university, and the outcome came to rest upon his putter, as he faced a 12-footer for par and victory and the adulation of his teammates. He also remembered Debby, the sophomore cheerleader he was trying to woo, and how he had hoped to impress her with an important win. As his memory sharpened and his Mind traveled back in time to that precise moment, dark clouds began to form in his head. He recalled vividly how he had missed that putt, pushed it long and wide and over the crest of the green to slide down to the fringe. He three putted and lost the match, and not long after the match he discovered that Debby was dating some surfer from California.

Back on 18, Mike's body hovers above the ball, but since his Self is divided by the absence of his Mind in the Present, he tops his putt and falls short, then three putts to ensure his place in the annals of mediocrity.

When a golfer makes *a Single Movement in Time...*

A golfer's Mind cannot be in the future.
A golfer's Mind cannot be in the past.
The golfer's Mind and body must harmoniously co-exist in the Present.
The golfer must be in the Now and in the Little Picture.
The golfer must be Present to win.

# PART 2

# THE TRANQUIL MIND

# HOME ON THE RANGE

*"Insanity is doing the same thing over and over
again and expecting different results"....*
*Albert Einstein*

We have seen what type of conditions lead to superlative play on the golf course even under excruciating competitive pressure. We have seen what it is like for a highly disciplined athlete to remain Present and harmoniously synchronized within himself to make the Single Movement in Time in a consistent way...consistent enough to shoot a 59.

There is no score to be recorded on the driving range, so we often make our best and most consistent shots there. If we play like pros on the driving range and blow up like grenades on the course, then we are establishing a routine for ourselves. The opposite would be better, but that is not the reality of the game. The reality is that we practice great. We trust in our skills, our innate capabilities, and the technological superiority of our clubs...and then we get on the course to play. Our bodies are suddenly no longer trustworthy, not to mention our clubs. There is an erosion of certainty. When these diminishing feelings become part of our routine, our sense of Self loses structure.

It seems that when we are on the driving range, it is much easier to perform our Single Movement in Time. We are not keeping score on the driving range, so that keeps us out of the future somewhat and helps us golf in the Present. Also, even though we would like to hit good shots on the range, we know in our heads that a good shot on the driving range basically counts for nothing, so we don't assign a lot of value to it. It is like living in the land of endless Mulligans.

"Sliced that one? Well here, try another!"

You are also not in a rush so your timing is not rushed as well. There exists the sensation that you are in your own space on the range, that you are not being observed and judged, except of course, by your Self. In fact, you are not really playing golf at all, just swinging away, a man standing in field swinging a stick.

Playing golf correctly means that you are able to maintain, through 18 long and often difficult holes, a cohesive sense of Self. That means an organization of experience that forms an emotional structure, and within that structure you maintain a positive and Self-regulated view of who you are.

# SELF-REGULATION

In order for a golfer to maintain an even keel or cohesive Self on the golf course, he needs to be able to Self-regulate. Since golf is such a solitary game, your internal Self Structure is all you have to rely on. No one else can do it for you. Not your coach, not your caddie, not your entourage, no one but you.

But what exactly is it to be Self-regulated?

Self-regulation refers to the ability to manage both *Expansive* and *Depleting* emotional states that interfere with a cohesive sense of Self. In other words, you want to resist Time Traveling into the future where your Expansive emotional state may be making you too excited about the prospect of a low score or a possible victory. You also want to resist traveling into the past where you may be subject to destabilizing memories and become emotionally depleted.

Self-regulation is the ability to return to the focus of your Mind/body synchronization after experiencing the debilitating Affect States of Anxiety and Tension. Whenever there is a disruption in a cohesive sense of Self, there are effects on Self-esteem, Self-agency, and the harmonious trusting between Mind and body. Self-regulation refers to the ability to maintain that cohesive sense of Self in the face of disruptive emotions and performance pressures.

An Expansion State relates to a state of excitement, an excitement that can occur when one's inflated sense of Self is momentarily rewarded. Like a balloon puffing up with air, your sense of Self has been expanded.

For example, a professional golfer who has just made a difficult birdie to the delight of the crowd must then overcome his excitement and calm down before teeing off for his next shot...which is tough to do when people are cheering for you. When the television camera points your way, and you know your image is being broadcast across the world, it is difficult to remain Present. This is an Expansion State, a state of excitement that is a great feeling, but takes your Mind out of your body. It is a state of overstimulation that may keep you from performing your Single Movement in Time.

There is a difficult par 3 in the Phoenix Open that is notorious for the crowd booing or cheering the golfer's performance to the green. If the golfer who has just birdied the last hole hits a bad shot on this scary par 3, the feedback is daunting. The bad shot stems from the excited state from his good performance just minutes before, and causes him to go from an excited state to a depleted state... from happy to depressed...just like that, in the blink of an eye, in the length of time it takes to swing a club. Going from an exhilarating high to a devastating low in just a matter of minutes, he becomes an emotional yo-yo. After his bad shot he enters a state of Self-depletion that will again need to be re-regulated before he attempts his next shot. He must try to get back into the Little Picture and his Single Movement in Time or he will continue to vacillate back and forth between Expansion and Depletion, between a feeling of joyous Grandiosity or eminent failure, between past and future.

Self-regulation is the management of de-regulating thoughts like Time Traveling, Swing Thoughts, as well as the flood of disrupting feelings like Anxiety, Tension, Self-depletion, Anger, and Grandiosity. But more importantly, it is the ability to sustain a feeling of well-being, of being comfortable within one's own skin. Being regulated is the sense that the Mind is firmly embedded in the body and can feel the unfolding of the body's motions as they occur.

The more firmly entrenched the Mind is in the body and therefore in the Present, the more information is exchanged between Mind and body when performing a complex task... like a Single Movement in Time.

# THE REGULATORS

As human beings we are amazing regulators. Being innately clever, we often seek to regulate ourselves by using fixes from outside our bodies. When we wake up in the morning, we try to manage away our drowsiness with a hot cup of coffee. Air-conditioners and heaters help us to regulate our core temperatures and keep us healthy and comfortable. Illegal and legal drugs help us regulate Anxiety and depression. We try to regulate our blood pressure and our cholesterol with pharmaceuticals. We diet to regulate our weight and visit the gym to regulate our fitness. Our nutrition levels are regulated through vitamin supplements and we eat chocolate to regulate our moods. We ride bikes, inline skate, and jog to help us feel more like our best Selves. We go shopping and we watch TV in an effort to calm our Selves down. We eat at fast food restaurants to fill the emptiness inside. We feel regulated, then de-regulated, and then make an attempt to re-regulate by whatever method fits our degree of need. When we drive home from the golf course, the bars that we pass along the way are jammed with people trying to regulate themselves after a long day of much de-regulation and energetic discomfort.

A great example of de-regulation and re-regulation is a person smoking a cigarette. A cigarette is usually smoked to satisfy a craving for nicotine, but there are other factors at play as well. When a person smokes a cigarette, what is their primary behavior? They breathe. They take long, often-exaggerated breaths, usually during a time-out situation from whatever they may be doing. Their actions are so engrained that the routine of smoking has stopped being a Left-Brained activity driven by mental instructions, but has become an automatic ritual through constant repetition. Smokers are often isolated, standing alone or sitting in front of their favorite ashtray, repeating well-worn actions in a ritualistic Right-Brained manner.

So what are we really seeing when we watch someone smoke a cigarette?

We are seeing a person who feels de-regulated... a person who's energy has become uncomfortable and is feeling out-of-sorts enough with himself to attempt to re-regulate themselves using a manufactured or processed substance from outside their bodies. They are really only feeling like themselves during the smoking process. When they are not smoking, they once again become de-regulated. Smokers are not Self-regulating... that is, they are not relying on their own Self-contained resources and capabilities to regulate themselves. They are inhaling a drug that is temporarily making their uncomfortable cravings and uneven energy disappear. But there is more going on than just the smoking of tobacco.

The smoker has separated himself from his fellow humans to seek a place to smoke alone or with a friend, so initially there has been the act of isolation. Then the cigarette is ritualistically plucked from its pack by well-trained hands without a thought.

So now the smoker has turned off the Left Brain and let the Right Brain become turned on. Then the smoker begins a practiced series of rhythmic breaths designed to calm and regulate the smoker's energy while allowing the busy Left Brain to rest and the Right Brain to take over the body's actions. So essentially, the smoker isolates himself, begins a familiar and well-practiced ritual, and through rhythmic breathing enters a state of meditation.

Buddhists, practitioners of transcendental meditation, and yoga students all use these same methods, except they leave out the part where they are inhaling carcinogenic smoke. Smokers and meditators are Re-regulating, some without even knowing it.

It is not unusual to see someone smoking on the golf course. Those players are Self-regulating with a little help from the tobacco companies. But for the most part, *the golfer stands alone* when he plays this challenging and beautiful game. Granted, the caddy may supply companionship and important advice about the conditions and tendencies of a course, but essentially, *the golfer stands alone* as he addresses the ball and sends it on its way. It is up to the golfer to be able to re-regulate naturally when he finds his mental and/or emotional energy getting out of control so that he can properly perform his Single Movement in Time. This means that the golfer must have a solid and flexible sense of Self that can bounce back and re-regulate after a bad shot or an unfortunate circumstance. There must be a vitality of Self that allows the unfolding of the golf swing under any conditions, including competitive pressure, difficulty of the course, and adverse weather conditions.

Remember, it was 102 unbelievably hot Memphis degrees when Al Geiberger shot his 59. He did not have an air-conditioned golf cart, was not taking miraculous Re-regulating golf drugs, was not being propped up by the cheerleading of a sports psychologist. What he did have was the ability to Re-regulate from shot to shot in super-humid conditions and continue to stay in the Little Picture to make his Single Movement in Time repeatedly in that perfect PGA moment.

As a golfer and a professional athlete, he stood alone.

# HEALTHY NARCISSISM

---

*"I'm the best and I'll thank you to remember that"*
*...Harry Vardon*

---

Narcissism has a bad rap. It is one of those terms that is widely misunderstood and generally evokes a negative response when it is mentioned in general company. One immediately pictures a vain and Self-possessed individual gazing at himself longingly in the mirror...Self-infatuation at its worst.

The term originated from a Greek Myth about a 15 year-old hunter from Thespiae who was famous for his handsome features. He was so proud of his own looks that he rejected the affections of all those around him, including romantic interests and even his own family. A nymph named Echo fell in love with Narcissus, but was rejected as well. One day when Narcissus was gazing at himself in a pool of water, Echo cast a spell on him and he fell in love with his own reflection.

Heartbroken by not being able to fulfill the phantom relationship with himself, Narcissus became listless and eventually transformed into the flower that is known by his name today.

Through this myth we learned about an overabundance of Self-admiration in humans and its harmful effects, and so the mention of Narcissism tends to bring up negative images that are frowned upon by the general population.

However, the above-mentioned trait is actually *Unhealthy Narcissism* and is only one side of the coin.

*Healthy Narcissism* at its core is the desire to be seen as eminently unique in the eyes of the Ideal Other... the Ideal Other being other people's valuation of you as an admirable human being. The Ideal Other is a concept within a person's psyche who can be a single person, like a parent, or can be a conglomerate of people, like a person's family, friends, spouse, coaches, and idols... such as Jack Nicklaus or Freddy Couples...a person who has value to you. Healthy Narcissism is the desire to shine in the eyes of those people who represent the Ideal Other, and to value yourself in such a way that you feel that you are worthy of their admiration. These people help you to formulate a set of values and ideals that can then act as an internal compass to guide you through life.

For example, a child named Mark is born to a family with the resources to support the career of a golfer. This baby, like any other baby, wants to think that he is the most special creature in the world to his mother. Immediately, the baby looks for the reward of his own Self-worth by looking for the delight in his mother's eyes.

In this case, initially the Idealized Other is Mark's mother, because for Mark, he wants to believe that he is the most special person in the world to his mother... and the infant constantly looks for this reassurance.

THE CHILD SEEKS THE MEASURE OF HIS SELF-WORTH
IN THE DELIGHT IN HIS MOTHER'S EYES.

As Mark grows and learns and eventually takes the golf clubs in his hands, his concept of the Ideal Other begins to change and grow as well. Later in life the Ideal Other becomes a conglomerate of his peers, heroes he has never met, and other people from within his life circle who he *needs* to value him as a person and an athlete. These are all people in his Mind that he has selected as a mirror of Self-valuation. In his head he values their opinions and desires to be loved, admired, or acknowledged by them. Eventually the Other becomes a set of norms, values, and ideals the player uses to measure himself and value himself.

As time passes, Mark learns his golf skills and personal skills and develops into a young man. At the core of his being, he still wants to shine in his mother's eyes, and now he increasingly seeks Self-valuation through the feedback he receives from the evolving Ideal Other. Mark's group that forms the Ideal Other now includes his parents, his sister, two of his friends that he plays golf with, the inspiring club Pro, and touring pros Jack Nicklaus and Tim Clark.

Mark is engaging in Healthy Narcissism. He is not spending the day gazing longingly in the mirror, nor is he mired in a Grandiose dialogue of internal cheerleading. Mark does not think the world revolves around him, nor does he imagine that he is the greatest human being to ever walk this land. Instead, like most of us, he wants to be seen as an adequate human being, to be seen as competent, that he has value, and that he is in fact worthy of being loved. Mark creates a picture of his own Ideal Self from within, mirroring the values of the people in his group that form the Ideal Other.

We must have idealized figures in our lives, and in order to reach our full potential, our performance must meld with the performance ideals that are inspired by the Other. Using his own selected group as a behavioral guide, Mark develops aspirations that are healthy, realistic, and attainable. In this way Mark has formed the basis for a good Self-image and healthy Self-esteem.

Mark's healthy Self-esteem manifests itself in the world in terms of performance that is satisfying and adequate for his ideals, where he feels good about himself, that he sees himself as worthy, and that he sees his behavior as being the type of behavior that would be appreciated by the Ideal Other.

Mark wants to shine at golf, wants to shine as a person, wants to embrace the core of Healthy Narcissism where it becomes the ultimate experience of Self, where his Ideal Self actually becomes his actual Self. In turn he can be viewed by the Other as being extremely unique and deserving of being loved.

Mark's Healthy Narcissism will lead him to a place where his ideal Self in fact becomes his real Self, and the Ideal Other provides the valuation for him. When he feels truly comfortable within his own skin, he feels merged with the calming and soothing effect of the acceptance by the Other. His competence at golfing and personal life skills helps form the basis for his healthy and enduring beneficial Self-esteem. Then Mark can truly say to himself, " I am worthwhile because my selected group of Others can see me as worthwhile."

The Ideal Other
Family, Friends, Inspirational Heros

Healthy Aspirations
&
Attainable Goals

# UNHEALTHY NARCISSISM

All human beings want to feel loveable, perceived as having value, and therefore deserving of love. To be idolized by other people is not pathological Narcissism, but a healthy liking of the Self by the Self, which represents a cohesive sense of Self in terms of how you value yourself and how you think others value you. That is the ideal.

---

*Healthy Narcissism is an important building block of the Self*

---

Unhealthy Narcissism, on the other hand, is a Mind-set that leads to problems. Unhealthy Narcissism is the type of Grandiosity that might encourage an elected government official to send photographs of himself from his phone while posing naked in the locker room. It is the type of Narcissism that allows a rock star who knows no boundaries to totally Self-destruct regardless of how his friends and family might try to rescue him. It is the public figure having an affair, justifying this diversion in spite of knowing that he is constantly being watched. It is an unrealistic vision of the Self that forms layers of Grandiosity to prevent him from facing the reality that his Expected Self and his actual Self are vastly different. He enters a world of Self-perception where he is "beyond" the realm and the rules of regular people.

*Unhealthy Narcissism,* made up of unrealistic Expectations, unrealistic goals, and overblown estimations of ability and capabilities creates the dangerous behavior magnet we call *Archaic Grandiosity.* The high from Archaic Grandiosity is like a drug, powerful and consuming, a tremendous magnetizing force.

# TOP OF THE WORLD

In 1949 James Cagney starred in the gangster classic "White Heat". It is the story of career criminal Cody Jarrett, a man whose partner in crime was none other than his mother. It is not a pretty story, as Jarrett spends time in jail and later learns that his father has died in an insane asylum and his mother has been shot in the back by Jarrett's own wife. A payroll robbery goes wrong at the movie's end and Jarrett ends up on top of a giant gas tank shaped like a globe for his final shootout with police. Hopelessly hemmed in and outgunned by police, Jarrett fires several shots into the tank below his feet, causing a massive explosion.

At this point, Jarrett joyously shouts the famous line: "Made it Ma! Top of the World!"

He is then engulfed in flames. Cody Jarrett's last words epitomize the behavior of a person with Unhealthy Narcissism, also known as *Archaic Grandiosity*.

# ARCHAIC GRANDIOSITY

> *I have often seen players attempt shots that
> I knew were impossible...*

There is no high like Grandiosity, as *White Heat* so dramatically illustrates. There is a tremendous feeling of entitlement when a person actually thinks the entire world revolves around him. It is called *Archaic* Grandiosity because it is a throwback to how we perceive ourselves as infants and how we relate to the world around us. A Grandiose person can remember when, as a small child, he thought the entire world emanated from around him. In fact, at that time, he felt he was the world itself...and the mother, the only mother that existed and the only mother that mattered in the world...she existed only for him, only for the child, and the mother and child were in agreement as far as how great and central to the world that they thought the child was. Such a mother would communicate to the child, " You are my prince. There is no other before you, as long as you are what I want you to be..."

Imagine that this child evolved very little beyond this belief, never stopped thinking he was central to the world.

And in order to keep up this false belief system, he had to constantly talk himself into it...and everyone else as well...thereby creating an interior dialog of Grandiose and reassuring comments.

We have all encountered this type of Grandiose personality in our lives. We see him in business and politics and in entertainment. Certainly we have seen him in competitive sports. He is the player who knows all and will be more than happy to tell you about it. He is the arrogant athlete, the braggart, the blowhard. Arrogance and Grandiosity are twin sides of the same coin. Yet despite all the rhetoric and show, it is not difficult to sense the underlying fragility of such a person.

Grandiosity is a defense against the underlying effects of inferiority, worthlessness, and inadequacy that a person may feel as a result of an inadequate and unhealthy development of the Self. It is a way of trying to regain Self-agency and maintain a level of performance. It is like an addicting and powerful drug to enhance an enfeebled sense of Self. Grandiosity is behavior that compensates for an inner feeling of inferiority by a smoke-and-mirrors illusion of superiority and greatness.

The Grandiose person is in fact doing an exaggerated impersonation of himself.

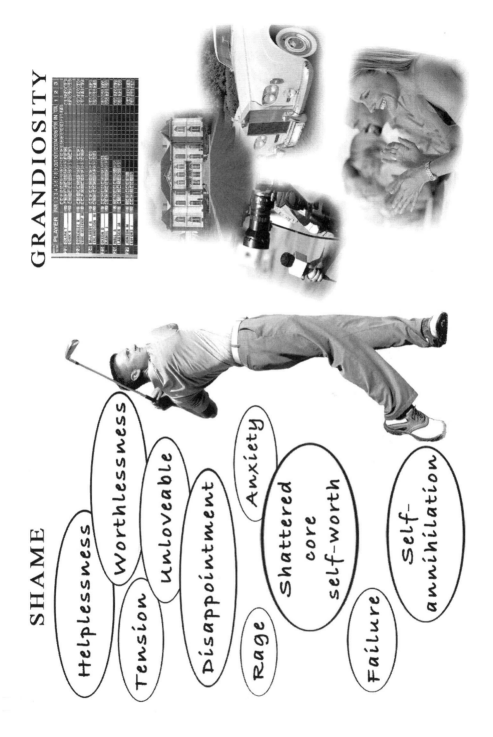

GRANDIOSITY

SHAME

Helplessness

Worthlessness

Tension

Unloveable

Disappointment

Anxiety

Rage

Shattered core self-worth

Failure

Self-annihilation

To maintain such an impersonation, the Grandiose individual must create a False Self that he constantly props up with an internal dialog of Self-praise. Eventually, through constant reinforcement, the false Self becomes the real Self and the real Self becomes a source of Shame. In spite of constant reminders from the real world in the form of failures, the internal dialogue will continue to set things right in order to maintain the false Self and its deftly crafted Grandiose image. In the end, the inner dialogue will dominate and overcome the annoying reminder of realistic external input .

Sam Vakmin put it this way:

---

*" A narcissist will always prefer his false self over his true self. No one can convince the narcissist that his true self is far more loveable and intriguing than his grandiose, inflated false self."*

---

If a Grandiose professional golfer were to find himself in the woods facing a shot that looked like an arboreal pinball machine, he would be reluctant to play the safe shot... to chip back low under the branches into the fairway or to take a stroke. Instead, he would choose an heroic shot that penetrates the dense tree limbs and climbs above the adjacent sand trap to land softly on the green near the flag, and perhaps even wander into the hole.

He would say to himself, " If I make this unbelievable shot, then my fans will see that I am the greatest golfer ever and I will become famous for pulling off this miracle of a golf shot."

The player then addresses the ball, hits it with all his strength, aiming for the small but alluring slice of blue sky through the trees. The ball accelerates off his clubface and ricochets off the nearest tree, burying itself deeper in the woods and drawing a groan of disapproval from the crowd.

Automatically he experiences Self-depletion in the form of depression and must somehow re-regulate before attempting his next shot out of the trees. It is not unusual for the Grandiose golfer to remain in the woods, carding a 12 after a promising string of pars and birdies. Should the golfer actually pull off the miracle shot, it could set him up for a further collapse of the Self, for the underlying structure is perilous. Like Icarus flying too close to the sun, he has all the farther to fall when his wings burn off.

Golf is a relatively safe game in which a disastrous Grandiose shot can happen and then be overcome. Granted, the ball could hit the tree and then rebound back into the forehead or groin area, but generally speaking, most golf rounds are survivable.

On the other extreme, a dangerous sport like car racing leaves no room for Grandiosity. The Grandiose personality's life expectancy on the racetrack is limited, typically crashing and killing himself and others through his overblown view of his own talents and capabilities.

# ANXIETY

At a college tournament a young and promising golfer named William Robinson was ready for his second shot. Will was a great athlete, tall and lanky with a smooth and powerful swing, and he had just hit a three hundred yard drive onto the right shoulder of fairway. He was the number one player on his college team and they were competing for a spot in the national championships. A great ball-striker, Will found himself out 160 yards with a comfortable lie. The pin placement was favorable, a reasonable distance from the water hazard looming on the right. He had played this course a hundred times and knew it like the back of his hand. He was one up over his nearest opponent and a birdie here would stretch the lead as they neared the club-house. Recognizing the importance of the shot, not just for himself, but also for his teammates and his school, he approached the ball.

The great magnet of Grandiosity drew Will into the future, and in his Mind he could see his shot landing next to the hole for a gimmie putt and the resulting birdie... then the closing of the match, two up, and the celebration by fellow players and coaches. The team would qualify for the nationals, breaking a seven-year drought, and Will would return to school as a sports hero, and all would be good with the world. Will's Grandiosity was drawing him into the future. Then, without even realizing it, his Mind bounced back into the past like the little square dot in a video game.

A strange and unwelcome feeling washed over him. Somehow, from an undefined source, a sense of dread and uncertainty invaded his Mind-set. Particularly shocking was the knowledge that only moments prior he had been relaxed, confident, and happy. But now he felt overcome by this wave of feelings.

His body, reacting to the threat, responded with the physical characteristics of fight or flight. Will's heart began to beat faster, his blood vessels dilated, adrenaline secreted into his bloodstream, and his muscles Tensed like springs. His awareness became nervously acute, senses keenly on alert... as if a voice had suddenly whispered, "Danger Will Robinson". He became completely de-regulated.

What was particularly odd was that Will was in one of the safest places on the earth. Other than the threat of lightning or the very occasional alligator lurking in the water hazard, there was nothing even vaguely threatening on this vast sanctuary from the modern world. So in the midst of all this safety, how was it that Will was being overcome by a wave of debilitating fear and uncertainty?

What Will was feeling, and what many golfers feel in this situation, was a wave of Anxiety. It manifested itself in the form of muscular Tension and disruptive emotions. To add more uncertainty to the situation, Will does not know where these disturbing feelings are coming from.

Anxiety can be defined as a psychological and physiological state that creates feelings of fear, worry, uneasiness, dread, and physical Tension. This mood condition often occurs without any identifiable triggering stimulus. That is the real problem with Anxiety. We usually cannot discern its origin and its reason for occurring.

The source of Anxiety for people in their daily lives and for golfers as well, is like the earthquake on the ocean floor that causes a tsunami. Like the tsunami causing a flooding of water, Anxiety causes a flooding of emotions. Whereas the tsunami is generated by unseen forces below the water, Anxiety on the golf course is caused by unidentifiable sources below the surface of the player's psyche. Just like the unfortunate tourist on the beach during a tsunami, the golfer does not care to address the cause of the thing that threatens him. He just wants to get away from it and he wants to get away from it immediately.

# EXPECTATIONS

*" I dreaded going to the tournament from the first tee to the finish. I constantly worried that people would think that I was weak. When I went into the locker room I kept my eyes on the floor and wouldn't look at other players. I was afraid that they thought I was a loser. I felt I was a loser – if not just awful, and I still feel that way."*
...Top Professional Golfer at the peak of his career.

Aspirations are wonderful things. They are the stuff that dreams are made of, incentives that draw one towards greatness. Healthy Narcissism, the core experience of the Self that leads us to good Self-esteem, is driven by realistic and attainable *Aspirations*. Even an attempt at fulfilling our *Aspirations* makes us feel whole...motivated people who are happy being exactly who we are and no more.

Expectations are a whole different animal altogether.

---

### *Expectations Are Killers of a Good Golf Swing*

---

Expectations are all about making realistic or unrealistic goals or performance ideals and linking the outcome to our Self-worth. In other words, if you expect a tremendous amount from yourself, especially in terms of performance on the golf course, you might form ideals about what is possible to achieve. These performance ideals may be beyond your capability and perhaps even beyond human capability. It is not just exhausting trying to achieve the un-achievable. It is the single most Self-annihilating behavior that one can initiate.

In fact, in our day-to-day lives, human behavior can be reduced to a formula based on the inability to fulfill Expectations. *The Life Formula* goes like this:

*THE TENSION GAP BETWEEN HOW YOU*
*PERCEIVE YOUR IDEAL SELF AND THE REALITY OF*
*YOUR A CTUAL SELF = THE MEASURE OF YOUR*
*UNHAPPINESS, ANXIETY, AND BODY TENSION*

It is the gap between the perceived actual Self and the perceived Ideal Self that produces Shame experiences, which lead to feelings of weakness, inadequacies, inferiority, and devaluation by the Self as perceived by others. If there is a discrepancy in our Minds between how we see ourselves and how we want to see ourselves...this is the perceptual gap that produces Shame.

---

### *Aspirations Do Not Define Our Self-Worth*

---

Aspirations involve the Self in the act of embracing a challenge or a task and then feeling worthy to meet that challenge or to perform that task. Aspirations are far different from Expectations. Aspirations do not define our Self-worth. Aspirations and their pursuit do not generate Shame.

You may also wonder what the difference is between Shame and Guilt.

There is a big difference in that Guilt is just a segment of behavior or thought. Guilt is something that springs from a particular incident, a breach of conduct, like forgetting a birthday or being unavailable for someone when they need help. With guilt, a person might say to themselves, " I've done something wrong and I look to the outside world for absolution."

---

*Guilt always looks for absolution and is not tied to your personal sense of worth*

---

A person who feels guilty might reason, "In this instance I feel like I have done something wrong, but I look to amend the situation and would like to make up for the instance that has caused my sense of guilt. I look to the world and to those I may have harmed for forgiveness. Yes, this thing that I have done makes me feel guilty, but at the same time this situation does not make me feel like I am a worthless or bad human being."

The person looks to the world to help absolve him from the sense of guilt. The person wants to connect with the world in a way that the problem is solved and his sense of Self is left intact.

A Shamed person, on the other hand, does not want to connect with the world and does not look to the outside world for absolution. The Shamed person wants to run and hide. Shaming is something we do to ourselves and is not imposed by the outside world. Being Shamed is the direct result of falling short of our own Expectations.

This is because Expectations *do* define our Self-worth.

---

*Expectations Define Our Self-Worth*

---

Expectations are goals that demand that you achieve them in order to feel worthwhile. They are goals that should or must be accomplished in order to please the chosen members of the Ideal Other and fulfill the qualifications for Self-worth. They are measurements of our own Ideal Self that we think should make up the basis for our Self-esteem and life's vitality. Expectations are the greatest killers of the vitality and healthy perception of Self-worth that give our lives richness and meaning. They are also the greatest killers of a good golf swing.

When a golfer has Expectations, Expectations that are intrinsically linked to his Self-worth and feeling of well being, then he is setting himself up for the depleting experience of Shame. If the golfer's performance falls short of his *expected performance*, then this discrepancy creates an energy gap between Expectations and the golfer's real performance...causing Tension and Anxiety in his body.

The more there is a discrepancy in our Minds between how we see ourselves and how we *want* to see ourselves... this is the perceptual gap that produces Shame.

Shame is a total body experience. If you feel Shamed, to you it means that your total person is defective, flawed, and inferior...and the response to Shame and the Vulnerability of Shame is to hide, to defend yourself at all costs against exposure as flawed and inferior individual. That's why golfers will do anything to avoid Shame either by affecting Grandiosity or falling into the helpless world of Self-depletion.

Self-depletion is the opposite of Grandiosity. Self-depletion is to see yourself and experience yourself as absolutely flawed, inferior, and unworthy of acceptance, love, or value...and to be seen that way by other people, especially those within the circle of your Ideal Other. A person with Expectations gives himself up to the Ideal Other, giving the

Ideal Other tremendous power over him, never realizing that the Ideal Other is something that he has created within his own Mind. The deeper that Shame affects Self-cohesion and Self-esteem, the greater the desire to control it...and the more Anxiety and Tension is created.

Take the *Life Formula* and apply it to competitive golf, and it goes like this:

THE TENSION GAP BETWEEN EXPECTED PERFORMANCE AND ACTUAL PERFORMANCE = THE MEASURE OF SHAME

Shame is " a painful emotion caused by embarrassment, unworthiness, or disgrace," caused by a failure to live up to Expectations.

This emotion often manifests itself in the form of depression. Most depressions are Narcissistic in nature, a depletion of your Self because you feel that you have not lived up to the Expectations of those in the circle of friends, family, and heroes who make up your Ideal Other. When the tension gap between reality and Expectations becomes elongated, the size of the tension gap equals the Measure of Shame.

When Shame invades the body, it shows up in the form of Tension and Anxiety. A player can flee from the Tense and Anxious feeling by shoring himself up psychologically in the false comfort of Grandiosity. He can reassure himself that instead of facing his fear of inadequacy and embracing the human condition, he can take a different road. The player retreats to Grandiosity and the illusion that he in fact meets or exceeds the imagined Expectations of his Ideal Other. His inner dialogue reassures him that he is "the greatest".

The other road, the road downward and opposite from Self-admiration, is the road to Self-depletion. This is a condition where the golfer feels devalued, incompetent, and unworthy of being seen as adequate or being loved by his imagined and selected group of Ideal Others.

---

*"I feel like I'm a failure as a husband, father, and a professional golfer. I feel down and listless like I have no energy. I really need help. I don't know what to do or where I'm going and if things don't change I'm going to quit the tour."*

...Professional Golfer after a disappointing tournament.

---

The symptoms of Self-depletion include passivity, lack of confidence, hopelessness, and withdrawal from the world.

A depleted golfer might feel numbness and inertia in the body, a lack of connectedness to his muscles, and a loss of tempo. Depression and Self-depletion *numb* the body.

These emotional states are caused by the elongation of the tension gap between imposed or Self-imposed Expectations and the realities of life. If the distance between what you expect from yourself and who you actually are is minimal, then the tension gap will only cause a minimal discomfort in the Mind/body connection. However, if the distance between the fulfillment of Expectations and actual performance is large, the resulting Shame will reduce the golfer to a blubbering mass of protoplasm. This phenomenon can be represented by a simple formula:

## THE SIZE OF THE TENSION GAP = THE MEASURE OF SHAME

This behavioral formula applies to every athlete in every athletic pursuit at some time in the unfolding of their careers. It is inescapable. There is no perfect golf swing. There is no perfect golfer. There is no perfect athlete. And even when the calmest and most experienced and talented of all golfers encounters a situation when their Minds begin to Time Travel back to a place where their Self-esteem is in jeopardy, when for a moment they lose trust in their bodies, then the formula for Shame comes into play. Then they lose communication with their bodies and cannot synchronize Mind and body to get back into the Little Picture.

The formula for Shame and the golf swing is a simple one. The more Shame a person experiences, the more that Shame energy is converted into Anxiety and Tension in your golf swing.

## THE MEASURE OF SHAME = THE AMOUNT OF ANXIETY AND TENSION IN YOUR SWING

One professional golfer was heard to say, " When I got to the last hole in the tournament, I was tied for the lead. Suddenly I lost all feeling in my hands. My body felt limp and dead, and I couldn't remember how to swing and I had no feeling for the club in my hands. I became very anxious and felt oddly alien and outside my own body, like a detached onlooker. I became frightened but had to step up to the ball and hit it, and the ball went way right and put me into trouble. Somehow I recovered somewhat, and I got my body to move a little better and was able to save par. But what frightened me most was not knowing or understanding why I suddenly felt that way...and then I was confused because I had no idea how I was able to recover".

These symptoms are typical of the numbing consequences of Shame. They are also symptoms that are magnified by the stress of playing at such a high level.

The higher the level of golf, the greater the stress that the player experiences.

As Expectations escalate, so does the potential for being Shamed.

Most people think they can never undo the things that Shame them. They never feel like they will ever feel adequate. When a golfer feels Shame, it infects every pore of the body, that cold icy feeling of despair and depletion that runs all the way down to the tip of your toes. Shame is the single largest de-regulator of the Self.

One professional golfer summed it up, " I am always trying to do what others expect me to do."

# THE TRANQUIL MIND

---

*"For this game, you need above all things, to be in a tranquil frame of mind."...Harry Vardon*

---

The Tranquil Mind is a Mind at peace in the Present with no psychological tug toward Time Traveling. For a golfer, it is a Mind free from Expectations, a Mind that is firmly imbedded in the body. It is a Mind immersed in a Single Movement, a singular unfolding of trained muscles trusted to perform in sequence and tempo. The Tranquil Mind is Tranquil because it is lacking an agenda.

I once knew a famous artist named Mary who lived in North Carolina. Talented and keenly intelligent, she lived according to a strict lifelong agenda that involved unreasonable goals and Expectations not only for herself, but for those around her as well. Although she was famous for her art, she was more famous for her cutting criticisms and unkind words. She was hard on herself, mercilessly cruel to her own daughter, and treated her daughter's husband like a pariah.

However, as Mary grew old, she developed a type of dementia that obliterated her long-term memory. In the process, Mary's agenda was forgotten as well. As her agenda faded, she no longer mentally Time Traveled into past disappointments or bounced forward into a future of worry, possible failures, and the pressure of Expectations. The demanding Ideal Other she had been pleasing all her life had faded as well, finally laid to rest.

Then the strangest thing happened. A lifetime of worry and bitterness, controlling behavior and cruelty...all fell away. Almost overnight, Mary became a delightful person. From that point on she overwhelmed people with her contagious happiness, her smile always beaming. She sang songs, made jokes, and made peace with her long-suffering daughter. The two became great friends and even the husband was welcomed into Mary's new circle of loved ones. Mary was no longer hindered by a damaging past, but she still had a Present and a future.

Mary's experience is not a unique phenomenon. In a study of time perception in the 1970's, test subjects were given scenarios of hypothetical time frames while under hypnosis. The first scenario was simple and familiar.

The subjects were told, "You have a past, a Present, and a future."

As expected, there was little observable change in demeanor since this was the temporal arrangement the subjects were accustomed to.

Then they were told, "You have a past and a Present, but no future."

The subjects, without exception, became extremely depressed. Some were un-consolable and began sobbing. They were quickly snapped out of the trance to minimize their suffering.

In the next scenario they were told, "You have a Present and a future, but no past."

Now the reaction of the subjects was tears again, but this time they were tears of joy. There was laughing and hysteria, giddiness and glee.

In the final scenario, they were told, "You have no past and no future, but reside constantly in the Present."

The result was that the subjects took on a serene demeanor, grounded in satisfaction, comfortable in the peace of their Tranquil Minds.

For a golfer, to reside in the Present is to reside in the interior of the glass dome, performing A Single Movement in Time. This is the golfer who is anchored in the Now, not Time Traveling into the Shameful past or the Grandiose future. This is the golfer at peace with himself, at peace with the outcome of his movements. This is the golfer with the Tranquil Mind.

I always chuckle whenever I see the vintage photograph of Harry Vardon teeing off with his beloved smoking pipe in his mouth! There was a man in his element, a man with a Tranquil Mind, a player who was Self-regulated. But no matter if you are a golf legend or a weekend player, something will happen at some time to make you feel de-regulated.

When a player finds himself de-regulated, there are some techniques that can minimize or eradicate feelings of Anxiety, Tension, and the lack of focus caused by Time Travelling. These exercises will restore your concentration, get you back into the Present, and back into your body. Then your Mind and body can re-synchronize so that you can actually *feel* your well-trained and trusted body functioning perfectly again. Ancient monastics called it, "Returning to the Breath."

# BREATHING

The first thing you need to learn is *how* to breathe. I know that sounds like a quote from an old Kung Fu movie, but truer words were never spoken. We are used to breathing basically one way in our normal lives, which is to inhale through the nose into the *upper* part of the lung and chest. This type of breath certainly keeps us alive, but does not use the entire lung and thereby does not provide as much oxygen. The first thing that happens when a person is deprived of oxygen, even a little, is that they feel Anxious. When a person feels Anxious, fight or flight reactions cause muscular Tension. Some people are shallow breathers and feel Anxious or worried all the time. Nothing ever seems quite right. There is always something wrong.

Worry, Anxiety, muscular Tension, and a negative viewpoint are huge debilitators of the golf swing. These are all aspects of the Big Picture that can keep us from being totally linked in Mind and body, and therefore not in the moment.

To Regulate the way we feel as golfers after we hit a bad shot, we must realize that we are Vulnerable to all of these negative Affect States and be ready to minimize or eradicate them. The best way to initiate this process is by breathing in a way that calms us down. The following abdominal breathing method will begin the process of calming the body down so that you can feel totally synchronized in the Present and ready to make your *Single Movement in Time.*

1. Inhale into your abdomen through your nose.
2. When your lower lung is full, expand upward into your chest.
3. Breathe out through your mouth. Really let it go.
4. Take four, and only four breaths, as above.
5. Take the time to feel the relaxation, the decrease in Anxiety, the lessening of muscular Tension.

If you hit a bad shot and start to experience emotional flooding or distracting thoughts, you can do your four breaths while you are walking to your next shot. Or if you are on or near the putting green, you can calm yourself with rhythmic breathing while waiting your turn, or while waiting your turn by the side of the putting green.

Tiger Woods, when he was at his best, could be seen on the side of the green with his eyes half-closed, Self-regulating in preparation for his putt.

This is an immediate way for golfers to initiate Self-hypnosis, which is really just a way of becoming very calm, relaxed, and concentrated.

After your four breaths (and only four breaths) you can begin to scan your body, looking for areas of muscular Tension. For golfers, the primary concern would be the arms and the muscles of the upper back and neck, because Tension in these areas leads to a fast swing. In the act of scanning, you will become aware of small pockets of Tension in various parts of your body, and just the act of awareness can help you to let it go. When you feel calm, when you have returned to the Present, then you can return to golf.

It is a natural Transition when you have been calming your body that your Mind can then stay "in the moment" as well. And your Mind and body will automatically synchronize in the Present when you return your attention to golf.

## Feel Your Body and Mind in the Present Moment

This is when we Transition into the first of our gifts, the Practice Swing. In the Practice Swing, the golfer can feel his Mind and body operating in the moment of the swing, so his focus and feeling awareness are all in the Present.

Focus the Mind and body on the Practice Swing so you are aware of nothing but the Practice Swing because that is exactly the movement you want to replicate in your actual swing. The more you turn the task over to your body, the better off you are. Your body is so smart that it may choose to hit an entirely different shot from the one you mentally chose. Let the body take over.

Once you are satisfied with your Practice Swing, you can address the ball. If you feel uncomfortable over the ball or you feel muscular Tension, that the shot is just not right, use the second of your two gifts...Step Away From the Ball. Just the knowledge that it is all right to Step Away From the Ball makes the shot-making process less stressful. After you Step Away From the Ball, you can take another Practice Swing to get back fully into your Right Brain and connected with your body in the Present. Some top players in the past had idiosyncratic shot routines that they would need to start over again after Stepping Away From the Ball. That's fine, as long as you are able to return to the Practice Swing with a clear Mind.

Address the ball again. Scan your body for residual Tension. Your consciousness has already switched from the Left Brain to the Right Brain, the side of your brain that is in direct contact with your body. You are able to *feel* the flow of consciousness within your body's movement. This is the Mind/body synchronization that produces your smoothest swing. You allow the movement to unfold...no Expectation to fulfill, no uncertainty to overcome, no score to post... just the beauty of a golf swing unfettered by outcome...

## The Single Movement in Time

No one is more superstitious, or magic seeking, than golfers. When primitive people experienced problems, they would seek the help of a shaman. As a quick fix the shaman would give them a potion or amulet to protect them or empower them. Today when a golfer goes to a golf shaman, the shaman gives them a giant putter. That is why golf gurus and teachers tend to last only one season. If a golfer doesn't get immediate results, he leaves... after two sessions. Then he will seek another quick fix or another technique.

A golfer must not give himself up to a technique or a quick fix because he will then experience powerlessness from relying on the technique rather than being able to do it himself. A golfer becomes a model for a loss of Self-agency simply by desiring a technique.

What happens to a golfer when he hits a bad shot? If he is Vulnerable to Shame, he is immediately overwhelmed by a feeling of powerlessness, worthlessness, and the feeling that there is not a thing in the world he can do about it... which is terrifying...but if he has a solid sense of Self, he can just absorb it, re-regulate, and move on to the task at hand. It is this inner Self-structure that allows him to re-regulate immediately.

Of course...if you are in the middle of a golf game and things go wrong you don't want to have the inner dialogue that says, "Oh, this must be coming from me not regulating my narcissistic Self-state very well, and thereby destroying my Self-object functions". That is not what a golfer wants to be thinking on the golf course, regardless of how important it is that the golfer seeks to understand themselves.

A professional athlete once said to me, concerning the flooding of destructive emotions, "I don't know where it comes from, and I don't know what causes it. I just know it is awful, and I just want to get rid of it."

Ultimately the overwhelming flood of emotions distills into one feeling...a feeling of powerlessness. For a golfer this sense of powerless can be a driving force towards Self-regulation. Golfers fear a sense of powerlessness. Golfers are usually raised comfortably with a resulting good and constant sense of Self-agency, so when they lose it, they are truly lost. It would be like taking away food and water. Having a cohesive sense of Self for a golfer is like being able to breathe oxygen. A cohesive sense of Self is as necessary to a good golf game as calming oxygen is for the body. When all the elements of Self are working correctly, they vitalize and enhance who you are as a human being.

As you begin your quest to stay in the Little Picture while playing golf, you must become a master of the Regulation of your Self. In our development as golfers we may have formed an Ideal Other that is no longer applicable or is outdated. You may have a brother, for example, who you thought was really cool as a kid, and that his opinion of your projected success was important to you...you may have seen him as having *Expectations*...perceived emotional demands that may have been necessary to your Self acceptance. But just as your life has changed, his life has changed as well, and your perception of his life has changed. One day you see that your admiration for him has diminished and that he is not someone you still admire, and that you in fact now only tolerate him, so he can be dropped from your Ideal Other. Your concept of the Ideal Other can change to something more realistic and attainable. It is possible to rearrange your Ideal Other or update it to a group that fits your Present life and your reassessed aspirations...hopefully a group not linked to Expectations. This will help minimize the gap between your Expectations and your actual Self. The smaller the gap, the happier you will be...and the more you will feel like your true Self.

There is no substitute for the internal work that should be done to recognize a healthy Ideal Other and a realistic Self Image.

We are truly alone on the golf course. And as much as we involve ourselves with relationships and possessions and the hope that our lives will be filled with joy, we are in fact alone in life as well. We are solely responsible for the maintenance of our integrity. It has been said, " Man is born broken. Love is the glue that holds us together."

I would like to think that we are *not* born broken, but rather that we are born Vulnerable to fragmentation as we journey onward from childhood, and that love is the glue that then holds us together. It is not just a love from the outside world, from our family members, from our friends...but a healthy love of our own Selves that helps us to grow. We do not have to stay fragmented. We have the power to change our Aspirations and Expectations, to choose to live in the Present, and to do all things in turn as a *Single Movement in Time.* When we accept who we are and how we developed and who we would realistically like to be, we can rest comfortably in the company of our own

Selves. This is the work of our lives, to recognize who we really are, to see that our Selves are worthy of being loved and are competent, and then embrace and maximize that sense of interior wealth.

# QUESTIONS AND ANSWERS
# WITH DR. WADDINGTON

Q. What part is played by the Ideal Self?

A. It is the way we would like to see ourselves...our best Self, the way that we think people will then approve of us... and the way we approve of ourselves, and the standards we establish for the Ideal Self, performance wise, in order to be acceptable to ourselves, and what we project to be acceptable to others. Anything less than this forms the gap between how we wish we were and how we really see ourselves as being...that tension gap is what produces the debilitating Affect State of Shame and feelings of power-lessness.

Golfers want to be seen a certain way. They want to be seen as special people, that they are great, that they have value, that they are worthy of being admired. When they hit a bad shot, how do they perceive themselves and how do they perceive the way others see them? Golfers have very flexible emotional states. As Bobby Jones said, "One moment soaring, falling the next..." It is crucial to be able to find a middle ground in this emotional tempest. If they cannot stay in the middle, if they fly too high or too low, then Tension and Anxiety will enter their bodies...Tension and Anxiety that are caused and fueled by Shame.

Shame is the driveshaft that produces negative emotional states in golfers under pressure.

A golfer often sees the origin of Shame as coming from outside of himself. Golfers are not in fact <u>being Shamed</u>, but are <u>Shaming themselves</u> by their failure to live up to the Expectations of the Ideal Self. In their hopelessness, they fail to see that the Ideal Self and the Ideal Other have been created by their own choosing and their own design. With failed Expectations, they are unable to have Self-affirmation after making a mistake, and once again become Vulnerable. As I've often said, "Expectations are not just the killers of a good golf swing, they are the killers of a good life."

Most golfers don't want to deal with anything other than the unintended consequence of Vulnerability, which is Tension. They do not want to address the cause of the Tension: fear of Vulnerability itself. Golfers use many techniques to relax themselves, but ultimately these techniques cannot work unless they actually address Shame Vulnerability as the source of Tension. They will stay Vulnerable, and rarely understand what it is that makes them feel Tense in the first place. They feel like what is happening to them is coming from the outside, and that there is nothing they can do about it. They never realize that the pressure is not actually *imposed* on them, but in fact has been imposed by themselves through Expectations.

Q. Golfers get impatient for a solution...may even *expect* one...

A. The golfer wants a solution *immediately*, wants it simple and wants it to be infallible. So when the cameras are pointed at you, everyone's watching, what are you gonna do? Worry about hitting the shot or Shaming yourself? It's very hard to focus on what you need to do to stay in the Little Picture and hit a good golf shot.

When a pro golfer feels ashamed of his performance, be it only one shot, he cannot function. His Shame comes from being unable to fulfill Expectations and the result is physical, psychological, and emotional Tension. Even if he uses relaxation techniques to alleviate the Tension, he can tell that the source of this energy is still there, and he feels like he cannot function...and he is right. This is when an *Anyway Shot* occurs in an attempt to get the shot over with and the Tension as well.

What Shame does is that it interrupts a cohesive sense of Self. Without a cohesive sense of Self, the Mind and the body cannot function in a synchronistic way in the Present. Shame interrupts the process of Mind/body communication. Then a person is left with Self-doubt, feeling flawed, and lacking healthy Self-agency. He's defensive and he then introduces the greatest physical debilitator to a great golf swing—Tension.

Q. What about Vulnerability?

A. There is no Vulnerability like Shame Vulnerability, because it is the Vulnerability of Self-annihilation. Shame annihilates your positive sense of Self. Fear of the annihilation of Self, being exposed as flawed, as someone who others will look down on, someone who does not measure up to Expectations...that is the depleting power of Shame. And Shame has consequences:

First, you are incredibly Vulnerable to Shame. This fear of Vulnerability is the source of Tension and Anxiety in the body.

Secondly, you are Vulnerable to being Re-shamed which is worse than the first, because your Vulnerability has already been tested and found to be wanting. It is the proverbial salt in the gaping wound.

Vulnerability to Shame makes you bounce back and forth between past and future, knowing that Tension inhabits the body.

Both are experiences that golfers have. No one is immune to them. There is no such thing as a perfect swing that will make a golfer immune to Anxiety and Tension. Because of Shame Vulnerability, the resulting Tension and Anxiety are so debilitating, a golfer will do anything to defend against experiencing these Affect States. If you don't feel threatened, then there is no reason for your brain to create Tension in your body.

Q. But golfers tend not to address the source of the problem?

A. Golfers and other athletes want to deal with the symptoms, the Tension, the Anxiety, the loss of feel and the resulting numbness, the absence of tempo. They want to eliminate the symptoms and then they think they will be bulletproof. So the golfers spend endless hours on the practice range trying to relieve the problem, forgetting that what happens on the practice range often stays on the practice range, and that their problems are caused by the Vulnerability from Shame that they experience in competition when they stop trusting their swing. Since the cause of the problem is not being addressed the problem continues...a fragmented sense of Self. The golfer must never separate his body and his Mind. He must always stay in the moment, in the Little Picture. There is no match, there is no score, there is no reward in the future, no embarrassment from the past...only the moment, and a *Single Movement in Time.*

Q. And when we get out of the Little Picture?

A. As intelligent evolved creatures, we *think* more than we actually make movements. So it is not unusual for us to become Vulnerable to destabilizing thoughts when we are trying to make movements. When we have negative thoughts that destabilize us, and we become Tense and Anxious, where does our focus go at that moment? Our attention is magnetized away from hitting the ball and concentrates instead on our nervousness. Unfortunately, the Mind cannot be focused on two places at once. It just cannot do it. When the destabilizing force is Present, be it Tension or Anxiety, the Mind can only focus on the nervousness and nothing else. It becomes literally impossible to focus on the Little Picture and make a Single Movement in Time.

Q. People tend to play games with themselves?

A. People like to fool themselves, to go with the more comforting pretensions of denial and distancing themselves from the Vulnerability that is causing them so much discomfort. Most people want to run away from, avoid, and disassociate from Tension. If you can't avoid or run away from the problem, disassociation is your only option.
For instance, if a guy were to go into a graveyard at night by himself, he might start whistling a happy tune to disassociate himself from the obvious fear he felt from being in that spooky situation. A golfer will fool himself in similar ways, saying " Yeah, I'm feeling great," or "I'm gonna birdie this hole," when actually he knows that he is anxious and fearful and is in fact just whistling in a graveyard.

Q. And Shame is a consequence of trauma when we feel Vulnerable and we are faced with fight or flight?

A. Actually, genetically what we have built into us is the desire to protect ourselves: One way is to fight, one way is to flee. Either way the key aspect is the protection of the Self. In modern times, in the game of golf, it is a reaction to protect us from Vulnerability. Often a golfer will rush through a shot, just to get the motion over with, just to hit it "anyway". This is a flight reaction. What we are really talking about is how to keep a cohesive sense of Self, what happens to the Self when it fragments, and how you can put it back together again. This is not just about golf. This is a paradigm study for all of "Self psychology." When a person understands the principles of keeping a cohesive sense of Self, of re-regulating when the Self fragments, of staying in the Present, when the past and the future beckon, it is like an introduction into his true relationship with the world. It is like the fish that jumps out of the water and says, "Oh, that's what I live in."

Q. But Anxiety could destroy that consciousness in a flash...

A. Consciousness has to return to the body itself after a bad shot creates Anxiety. The Mind and body must be re-synchronized. When Tension is present, the Mind and body are never synchronized. The same thing can happen with Grandiosity. After you make five birdies in a row, the Mind travels into the future for the next birdie, and boom... disaster strikes. Occasionally Grandiosity pays off in the form of a risky shot that fares well, for it is a rare occurrence, and the gambler within us is seduced by intermittent reinforcement, the most powerful kind of reinforcement, just like the empty-pocketed Vegas flop. The *Anyway* shot is the same thing. One pro golfer told me, "I don't think I ever hit an *Anyway* shot with a good result. If I did, it was just a fluke or lucky." Not good as a steady diet of how to play golf.

Any kind of overwhelming state can cause Performance Anxiety. Overstimulation does not have to come only from a negative state or a bad result. It can also come from a "top of the world" emotion and the resulting futuristic Grandiosity. Overstimulation either way is a negative. That's why in golf psychology, "Pumping yourself up" with cheerleading positive thoughts actually creates an undesirable Affect State. You need to be in the middle, like the Buddha would recommend... not too high, not too low.

In order to not feel inferior, the Grandiose personality pumps himself up by saying "I'm really great! I am the best. Nobody can beat me." He identifies with the Grandiose image of himself, which is really a defense against the nulling products of Shame, whereas if he were really honest with himself, he would admit that he feels inferior or inadequate.

If you just stood in a meadow with a stick and a ball, as the old saying goes, which is what golf really is...then you wouldn't care if the ball went near or far, high or low, right or left. It just doesn't matter, so the hitter does not experience Tension. In fact, he experiences elation from the sheer joy of that unfettered *Single Movement in Time*. Isn't that why we play anyway? It's about playing. It's about a celebration of the Self in physical motion and the joy that this game gives us.

Q. As long as we don't get overstimulated...

A. A good example of overstimulation is in tennis. You often see a female tennis player jumping up and down to get themselves psyched. Some of the men do it too, but mainly it is pervasive in ladies tennis. This jumping up and down and Self-psyching only creates a faster heartbeat and an overly excited mental and emotional state, when in fact the players should be doing exactly the opposite... they should be calming themselves down.

An athlete can calm himself down from Anxiety fairly quickly, like the basketball player who has been running up and down the court and is suddenly fouled. When he steps up to the line for his foul shot he immediately begins to calm himself down. He takes deep breaths. He bounces the ball in a ritualistic way. He disassociates himself from the chaos around him to focus on his goal. Only then does he release the shot....a *Single Movement in Time*.

Q. What about the Transition...the pause in the middle of the backswing?

A. If you ask a good golfer where he will have a problem with his swing, he will invariable say, "In the Transition, at the crucial moment at the top of the backswing". The Self has to be coherent enough, at the pause at the top of the swing, to tolerate the unknown, which is really what the Transition is. If you are caught up or magnetized by some form of Left-Brained gymnastics, past or Present, you will automatically introduce Tension into the swing that follows. Tension is the body's way of saying, "I am out of balance." It is the body's way of saying that the Self does not feel cohesive.

The ability to trust your body to perform what you have trained it to do, to allow yourself to be suspended, unhindered by time and behavior magnets, is the epitome of the great golf swing. The only way to make this happen is to be in the Little Picture, absent of fragmentation, with a full trust in the trained body. The Self has to be cohesive enough to tolerate the slow unfolding of the tempo sequence within a person's interior space...within a person's Self. This trust will allow that incredibly slow and elegant unfolding of the swing.

Q. Tell me more about this kind of trust.

A. As everyday people, we let go of our egos at night so that we can sleep with the supreme confidence that we will wake up in the morning. We go about our daily lives thinking and believing that we don't have cancer, or that we are not going to have a heart attack, and we are not going to be run over by a car...we will, in fact, continue to breathe... all based on an assumption with no guarantees. There are absolutes in our lives, particularly absolutes of perceived safety, that we take for granted and rely on for our Selves to operate with comfort in an unpredictable world... in our own sense of the Archaic Grandiosity of our daily lives. It is deeply ingrained in our core Selves, the belief that nothing is going to come out of the blue to interrupt this perceived cushion of safety.

Dribble that idea down to the golf swing, and you realize you must have enough trust in the body that it can do what you want it to do without any help or interference from the Mind.

When Tiger was at the peak of his game, beating everyone, his perception of the movement of his body was clear, and he voiced it in words that will forever be the quintessential statement about performance.

" I try to never let my mind interfere with what my body is trying to do."

Tiger trusted his body implicitly, so his ability to Self-regulate was almost immediate after a bad shot. When he was at the top of his game, he knew that trusting the body was everything. He never mistrusted his swing.

Q. And through mistrust of the body, the Mind can bring Tension into the swing?

A. Any kind of Anxiety or Tension that is introduced into the body is always from the Mind trying to control things. The Mind tries to take over to prevent trauma in the form of Shame from occurring... ironically achieving the opposite effect. We developed flight or fight reactions in primitive times to ensure our chances of survival. These reactions, so deeply ingrained that they actually stem from our DNA, create extra energy and an excited state to enhance the ability to flee to safety...or stand and fight.

Suddenly it's modern times. We are relatively safe, unbelievably safe on the golf course, perhaps the safest outdoor place in the world, and fight or flight Tension is introduced into your psyche because you have learned to fear the possible trauma of experiencing a Shame reaction within yourself. This Tension has been introduced because the Mind, who thinks it is really smart, does not trust the body to perform the task that it has been trained to do, and like an older brother or sister or parent or teacher, tells the body just how to do it. We are not fighting for our lives playing golf, but we are fighting for our sense of Self, especially from being Shamed, and appearing incompetent, flawed. And there is very little support system. If you were to play football, or basketball, or hockey, if you messed up, team members would support you, tell you it was okay and that you are okay. When you began to deflate, they puffed you up. In golf, it's you, yourself, and possibly your caddie. A golfer is left to his own devices which makes things much more difficult.

Q. I sometimes hear you talking about weighted shots.

A. I constantly hear players and commentators talking about "scoring shots", or "pivotal shots", shots that were eminently crucial in a round or a match...three foot putts or individual placement shots that are central to the outcome of the golf tournament. These terms and ideas, to me, are misleading, and in fact run counter to the proper psychology of playing golf. There is no single underlying shot that is any more important than any other shot in a round. They are all counted as just "one shot" on the scorecard.

The value of any particular shot in a golf tournament or match can only be determined after the match is over. One can only look backwards, into the past, to assess any shot's particular value to the round. If a golfer attaches particular importance to a shot while he is playing, he will inevitably find himself in the future and thereby attach Expectations to the outcome. And Expectations take us away from the Tranquil Mind that allows for a good golf stroke.

Q. What happens when you get away from the principles that allow for a good golf stroke within the Little Picture?

A. If you get out of those principles, if you get out of the Little Picture, then you fragment your cohesive experience of the Self. This leads to certain consequences, such as Shame, and then you will get into either the past or the future.

Shame is a further feedback loop that causes further fragmentation and increases bodily Tensions. When you experience all kinds of negative Affect States, which are basically negative emotional states, it is because something has gone wrong in the way that you have performed the basic principles of what you have to do to play golf correctly.

Playing golf correctly means playing golf where you maintain a cohesive sense of Self...which is elevating, enriching, and positive.

From Shame, what are you left with? To say that you have a fragmented sense of Self means that you are flooded with negative emotions, Shame being one, but also you are flooded with Anxiety. You are flooded by fear, and above all, you are flooded by a sense of powerlessness. Shame may be the biggest product, but these are the by-products of Shame, and destabilization. You will feel powerless, you will feel Anxious, and you will be out of touch with the cohesive sense of Mind and body that you experience in a positive way.

Then the overarching concern is: "How do I get back?"

Typically, the golfer's immediate answer is to get back to golf, to turn his full attention to the task of golf. That's not right. When you are overwhelmed by negative Affect, or Anxiety that you cannot contain...emotional energy that you cannot integrate in a way that allows you to maintain a cohesive sense of Self, with the Mind/body united, in other words... you must get your Mind back into your body in the Present.

You must, for the moment, forget about golf. You must attend to the fragmented sense of Self and the overwhelmed body Affect (emotional body reaction). If you are Anxious, worried, and your Mind is going all over the place, and in some ways you can't even feel your body except as Anxiousness, then you must attend to fixing that and not worry about golf.

Q. To disassociate?

A. Disassociation, which has always been looked on as a negative thing by psychologists, is really a necessary way of conducting life. We all have to disassociate at one time or another. A disciplined person, when confronted with a distraction that disrupts his focus, must block out anything that might interfere with that focus. So the last thing you want to think about at that moment is concentrating on golf. Because what that will do is further reinforce the feedback loop of fragmentation.

The golfer thinks: "I've got to make a good shot here! I've got to get my friggin' wits about me so I can make a birdie."

That's the usual Self-talk, the usual internal dialogue.

That's what you *don't* want to do. What you *want* to do is to tend to the disorganization of the fragmented Self-state and the resulting flooding of Anxiety. You want to attend to that first.

So what you want to do is to learn to re-regulate the Self, to diminish the sense of trauma, to let go of it. So then you can re-establish a cohesive Self-state.

A. What can the golfer do to re-regulate?

Q. The first thing you want to do is calm the body down, to begin to regulate the negative Affect State of being flooded with Anxiety, Shame, or a sense of powerlessness. These emotional states should be your primary focus, not the golf shot you are getting ready to hit.

When I was in high school in a championship basketball game, my team was ahead by one point and I had the ball at half court. There was one minute left. I just stood there calmly, holding the ball and watching the clock tick down. There was pandemonium in the stands, people shouting and waving and jumping up and down. It was so loud you could hardly hear. But I was so focused on the situation before me that I heard nothing, remembering it later as a slow motion scene from a silent movie. This is the case where disassociation allowed me to be totally calm and Present and perform my best at the task at hand.

Q. So first the golfer needs to find a way to calm down?

A. A golfer wants to find ways to settle himself down, and one of the quickest ways to do that is through breathing. Very few people other than Buddhists and meditators know how to breathe correctly.

When you go to a Buddhist mentor or therapist, the first thing they teach you is how to breathe. Most people breathe like a smoker smoking a cigarette. This, of course, is a smoker's way of Self-regulating. However, it is an in efficient way of breathing, with or without the smoke. The other common way of breathing is called shallow breathing. This is a type of breathing that occurs only in the upper lung. The lower part of the lung, the part in the abdomen, is never engaged. Only a small part of the lung surface is used in shallow breathing. This type of breathing causes oxygen deprivation and a reduced capacity for being Present.

Q. The rhythmic breathing helps reduce Tension?

A. Definitely. For a golfer, it can be like a walking meditation, a way to calm themselves in the seemingly infinite time between shots. It can be done without anyone even noticing, and it allows the player to enter a state of Self-hypnosis, where his positive Self can re-regulate.

When the golfer calms himself down through breathing, he can then begin to scan his body for pockets of Tension. For a golfer, his primary concern would be his arms and the muscles of his upper back and the neck, because Tension in these areas leads to a fast swing.

In the act of scanning, you will become aware of pockets of Tension in your body. Just the act of engaging that awareness can help you to let it go. The act of scanning begins to bring the Mind back into the body and into the Now.

Once you have returned to the Present, you can return to golf. It is a natural Transition when you have been calming your body in that your Mind can then be in the moment. Then your Mind and body will be synchronized in the Present when you return to golf.

This is where we get into the Practice Swing. In the Practice Swing, and this is crucial, the golfer can feel his Mind and body operating within the swing, in the moment of the swing, so his sensate awareness is all in the Present...

Total focus...Now, in the Little Picture.

As you progress down the fairway, nearing the pin, you must increasingly rely on touch. The closer you get to the green, the more Practice Swings you should take because you need more and more feel as you get closer and therefore you have to be more precise with your feel.

Focus your Mind and body on the Practice Swing so that you are aware of nothing but the Practice Swing. The more you turn the swinging process over to your body, the better off you are. That is the essence of giving yourself up to your Single Movement in Time.

Q. How do golfers re-regulate themselves when they feel Anxiety or Tension states in their bodies?

A. This is a constant struggle on the golf course. After a bad shot or Tension causing event the golfer must step away from golf. If you are Anxious and you are aware of it, you have to detach your Mind from golf itself, and that is a difficult thing to do. You must put your conscious awareness back into your body.

A golfer must focus his attention on his de-regulated Self and his Tension-ridden body. This is the time to take four deep breaths. First breathe through the nose into the stomach and then exhale through the mouth. After doing this four times, scan the body to monitor Tension states in the body, particularly the shoulders, the forearms, and the hands. Then the golfer can return to the "felt" sense of his Practice Swing.

What is important to constantly realize is that Tension and Anxiety wipe out the Right Brain connection with the body. The Right Brain connection to the body is what we feel, our conscious awareness of the body... feeling, impulses, states of attention, our sensation of movement. When a golfer is Anxious, the Tension erases the Mind's connection to the body. That's when the golfer says, " I can't feel anything. I don't know what's happening to me. I no longer know what I am doing." Some players say that, "I feel like my brain just left my body," and in a sense it does. If Tension erases the Right Brain's connection to the body, the golfer has in effect lost his Mind...because he is no longer aware of any feeling in the body.

I recently had an interesting conversation with Tim Clark. I asked Tim, " If your swing isn't working right, how do you fix it?"

"I just move the parts of my swing around until they feel right."

"Well Tim, how do you <u>know</u> when it's right?"

"Because of the right <u>feel</u>. I know my swing is right (correct) when it <u>feels</u> right".

My conversation with Tim assured me that the correct swing is a Right-Brained feeling. In fact, <u>feeling</u> is the language of the Right Brain.

The only way a golfer truly knows his swing is through feeling his swing in motion. Knowing a golf swing in the Left Brain invokes swing thoughts, swing theories, and swing mechanics. Therefore, when a golfer is playing, the Left Brain is no place to go to correct the swing. Knowing a golf swing in the Right Brain invokes feelings of correctness. In other words, the Implicit Procedural Memory System gives the golfer the sense of a correct swing by a transmitted feeling from the Right Brain.

If a golfer doesn't have an awareness of the Right Brain connection to the body, then what? There is no way you can *feel*. Anxiety and Tension act like an eraser that wipes out any connection between Mind and body. That's why you must first breathe, then scan for Tension states, then return to golf, because only then can the brain reconnect to the body so it can feel something.

One pro golfer summed it up, "I never understood what Tension and Anxiety really do to your ability to feel movement. Now I know. They act just like a Mind eraser."

Tension and Anxiety erase short-term memory. Tension and Anxiety erase most higher-level cognitive functions. That is why the golfer must recognize these states and immediately step away from golf to attend to these de-regulated states.

# CASE STUDIES

## #1. THE GOLFER WHO MUST HAVE ONE THING WRONG ALL THE TIME

This is a golfer who can never have it right! One thing or multiple things must be wrong in his golf game at any given time. Sometimes it is his putting, or chipping, or some other aspect of his game. As we worked on curing one aspect of his game, another would quickly fall apart. The most memorable aspect was how completely his Self-organizing state would change under different circumstances. For instance, if he hit a bad five iron, it didn't bother him and he wouldn't dwell on it. He could immediately put it behind him with no damage to his sense of Self, and with no resulting Self-fragility. He didn't lose any sense of Self-agency or cohesiveness. But if he was faced with a three-foot putt, his sense of Self completely strayed. He immediately became very Vulnerable, his head went into the future and he tried to guide his putter. He became fearful about what other people thought about him.

"I felt completely screwed, like I was about to look like an ass. I thought people would see me as weak."

At first it was difficult to understand how his Self-states changed so rapidly...why something always had to be wrong with part of his game. How could he be so confident in every other part of his game and so completely

Vulnerable in one part? His golf performance reflected the extreme variability in his Self-state. As our work on his past continued, we discovered that his father was very quick to criticize his "laziness" when he did not want to go to the range and work on his game.

The golfer never felt as if he had worked hard enough on his game to deserve to really win. Even though he quite consistently won every junior tournament, he didn't really feel as if he had done enough to earn victories on the big tour. Therefore, he had an abundance of top ten finishes without a win. The Self-organizing principles, even though he was very talented, had not been enough to deserve victories. Also he had a deep resentment of authority telling him what to do.

This resentment manifested itself in the form of rebellion. So even things that he knew that could help his performance, like working out in the gym for example...he rebelled against. He found that he would play well for a while after he rebelled, but that would not last for long.

"I had to comply with a regime and I never do well when I simply do what someone else told me to do."

This complying and rebelling has led him into long or sporadic periods of time in which he did not practice or work on his game. This has contributed to his having a Self-organizing principle, (a way of seeing and experiencing himself) that he really doesn't <u>deserve</u> to win, that he hasn't done enough to <u>earn</u> the right to win.

As he became more aware that this destructive Self-organizing principle was in fact a way of complying with his father, it began to lessen its hold over the way he sees himself. The result has been a significant improvement in his performance and his attitude. Golf has become more enjoyable as has the rest of his life.

# #2 I'M ON A ROLL

"I'm on a roll, three birdies in a row—I could birdie all the way in!"

Until this time, the golfer has been <u>in the moment</u> with each shot. He was playing securely in the moment, and then he thought, "I'm on a roll". Then he thought he could make anything and everything. He got into the future, extremely Grandiose. But at the same time he felt extremely Vulnerable, that he could screw up at any moment. Then he was frightened of looking like an ass, weak and like a failure.

Here we see how a golfer gets Grandiose. "I can birdie all the way in", sets up Expectations which put his Mind in the future causing a split between the Mind, body, and Self. First he sets up the Grandiose Expectation in the future. This splits his Mind from the body, putting him into the future, resulting in a quick, short swing. Since Expectations are tied to Self-worth, poor outcome is sure to follow leading to Self-devaluation, Shame, and feelings of inadequacy. This, in turn, leads to an increase in Self-vulnerability.

Now the golfer is extremely afraid of what will happen with the next shot. Hence, he is now more in the future and is even more Vulnerable and subject to Self-devaluation. If this cycle is not interrupted it will lead to continued deterioration in performance. The golfer must return to the moment and his Single Movement in Time and stop focusing on the outcome. Focusing on the outcome was what drew him out of his body to begin with.

# #3. "HIMSELF,
# THE GRAND ONE"

"I expect to hit my golf shots perfectly. Good golfers hit most of their shots perfectly. Only losers hit poor shots."

This golfer automatically sets his Self-states around perfectionism and Expectations. This will automatically split the Mind from the body placing the Mind in the future and causing muscle Tension in the body in the Present moment.

To help this golfer you must help him separate his sense of Self from <u>the outcome</u> of a particular shot. Also you must help him modify his notions of perfection and Grandiosity. I do this by telling him that the Greeks used to see perfection as lying within Utopia. Utopia, however, derives from two Greek words that mean "No Place". Utopia does not exist and perfection does not exist. Therefore the idea of perfection does not belong in golf tournaments.

It is necessary to reiterate over and over that our own sense of Self-esteem must be separate from the outcome. We only have control of the movement of the swing <u>in the moment</u>. We do not really have control over the outcome.

Sometimes good swings lead to bad outcomes, and sometimes bad swings lead to good outcomes. That is just the nature of the game.

A golfer's sense of Self-esteem and Self-confidence must reside in his ability to make good movements in the moment on a consistent basis.

Simply stated, Self-esteem follows from a sense of competency in the body, which is really the ability to continually repeat consistent and flowing movements. If his Self-esteem is linked to consistent movements repeated in individual moments, the golfer will derive cohesiveness in his sense of Self and TRUST in his ability to repeat the same movements. His pleasure will be derived in the deep satisfaction that comes from competent execution of fluid movements, <u>not the results</u>. The results are ONLY gratifying at the end of the round. (The Big Picture.)

# #4 THE BLACK CLOUD

This golfer is one of the most difficult to treat. He comes with an <u>extremely negative attitude towards the future.</u> He is the one that bad things always happen to. He is always unlucky, while golfers who he sees as less talented get all the luck. He gets only bad breaks and the lesser golfers get only good breaks. He sees his career as filled with a lack of promise. He is pessimistic as to whether there will be a change for the better in the future.

In terms of playing golf, his Mind either gets frozen in the past with memories of disasters and bogies, or frozen in the future with promises of repetitions of the same dismal fate. His attitude is perpetually negative and extremely rigid. You notice that all the "badness" is projected into the external world. This sense of Self is very Vulnerable and fragile so there is little ability to look inward or want to take responsibility.

Because he looks to the outside world for blame, he also looks to the outside world for salvation. He is the type of golfer who becomes endlessly lost in swing mechanics and swing thoughts, who thinks constant practice will cure him.

He presents a tough exterior to himself and to others while inwardly harboring a deep sense of fragility, if not inferiority. Part of him likes to think he "knows it all" and comes across as very arrogant, while actually he most often feels alone, bewildered, and lost. Invariably he suffers from an extremely negative Self-organizing principle in which he thinks he is bad, worthless, and really undeserving of good outcomes.

Needless to say, this rigid personality style is translated into his golf swing. His swing is rigid, meticulous, and mechanical, but his tendency to protect his Vulnerable Self causes him to constantly get into the future, creating more Tension and more rigidity.

Because of his personality problem, his golf problems are best addressed by:

1. Trying to constantly get him into the Present with his Mind synchronized with his body.

2. Uncovering his harmful organizing Self-states to lend new flexibility to his swing and personality. Helping him understand himself in a different and new positive way that will loosen up his attitude and body freedom.

In most ways this is now a purely psychoanalytic case rather than a golf case. What makes for a pessimistic prognosis is the golfer's extreme defensiveness about looking into his inner world and Vulnerable Self-states.

# #5 THE GOLFER WITH THE INABILITY TO SELF-REGULATE HIS AFFECT STATE (EMOTIONAL CONTROL)

This particular problem is epidemic to tournament golfers. It is one of the most important psychological tasks a golfer must perform. In a nutshell, the problem is how to keep your emotions in check or on an even keel. Without constantly attending to the problem of our emotional states, getting too high or too low, we introduce a whole host of psychological problems into our golf swing.

If we get too excited our swing speeds up, our focus becomes dissipated and our ability to regulate the pace and sequencing of our golf swing diminishes drastically. Inwardly our conscious focus shifts to the future and gets wrapped up in outcome scenarios. Psychologically we feel as if we can not slow things down, and our bodies become alive with Tension, a sure way to get a short backswing and an over-the-top down swing. Shots that are hooked or blocked are commonplace.

The other side of the coin is if we get too down on ourselves. Our focus now is on our mistakes...the bogies, the three putts, etc. This causes the Mind to be split from the body and focused on the past. This usually occurs with negative thoughts and feelings directed at the Self. One of my golfers put it this way, "If I make a bad shot or make a bogie or worse, I immediately begin to trash myself, seeing myself as wimpy or a piece of shit."

The body also feels slow and sluggish. Our spirits feel devoid of passion and energy. Many golfers look to the end of the round as the only answer to their agony. A damaged sense of Self rarely produces a favorable golf outcome.

REMEDY: The way to remedy both conditions is to immediately focus on our emotional states (Affect States) and the Tension States in our bodies...NOT THE GOLF SWING! We want to get our focus momentarily away from golf and into our body states.

#1 Breathing four times and only four times. Breathe in through your nose down into your stomach and up into your chest. Breathe out through the mouth feeling the release of Tension through your whole body.

#2 Then focus inwardly on the different parts of your body where you feel Tension, particularly your hands, arms, shoulders, and chest. When you feel calmer and Tension free, and free from Self-talk, get yourself back into the Present moment and back to golf.

#3 Take a relaxed Practice Swing (with eyes closed if you like). Let your inner awareness be one of smooth tempo and sequencing of your golf swing. In other words, "Put your Mind in your body." When the Mind is embedded in the body, we allow ourselves to feel the body's unfettered movement throughout the swing.

This is what I think Tiger Woods meant when he said, "I never let my mind get in the way of what my body is trying to do."

There is an inner kinesthetic awareness of body-feel in the sequencing of the movements of the swing. The Mind never splits off from this ultimate connection to the body. It never is allowed to focus on the outcome or the target during the swing. This is what is meant by staying completely in the moment: when each golf shot is an isolated event within itself. This is what is meant by the synchronization of the Mind and body in the unfolding of the swing sequence. This is the Single Movement in Time. In my opinion, no one in the past has done this better than Jack Nicklaus and Tiger Woods.

Even for those golfers who have some awareness of Self-regulation, they see it primarily as only a preparation for the next shot. In reality, Self-regulation should be practiced at all times. A golfer should maintain an overall awareness of Self-regulation at all times.

Think of a picture of an ancient scale with a balance beam. On one end is the Grandiose high, while on the other end of the balance beam is the depressive low. The golfer has a center point on the middle of the scale by which he attempts to keep his emotions centered, never too high, never too low. This is Self-regulation.

If you have ever watched Tiger on the side of the tee in the past when another golfer was swinging, you would notice his eyes were hooded, as if he were relaxing or not focusing on anything. This is when he was entering a serious meditative state, to regulate himself. You may also have noticed that on the rare occasion when he hit a bad shot and then got angry (one part of being de-regulated) the emotion quickly dissipated and you never saw any lingering effects. Then he took his next shot. He had re-regulated himself immediately so that with the next shot his focus was completely within the moment.

This is what I think is so often referred to as being "in the flow" or "in the zone". The more you stay in this frame of Mind the better chance (maybe the only chance) that you have to play to your maximum ability.

# THE JOURNEY

*"I have known Dr. Preston Waddington for more than a few years now, and have seen him work wonders with players in allowing them to play to their ability level. His take on how to do this is rather unique compared to many other mental gurus, but I assure you if you work on his way of playing in the moment you will certainly play better when it counts most.*

*His thoughts on anxiety, shame, and grandiosity have helped me unde.rstand what is going on when players start to disintegrate as the heat is turned up.*

*I particularly like the pieces on Expectations and The Tranquil Mind. I hope you will adapt and adopt what you find in <u>The Now Golfer</u> and start to play the golf you were meant to."*

---

*Good luck on your journey.*
*Martin Hall June, 2012*

---

Martin Hall is a former European Tour player and current teaching professional. Recommended by Jack Nicklaus, he was named 2008 National PGA Teacher of the Year and has been in the top 50 of Golf Digest's Top 50 Teachers since its inception. Martin is currently the host of the popular Golf Channel show, "School of Golf".

# CLOSING THOUGHTS BY PLAYERS CHAMPION TIM CLARK

I've been working with Pres Waddington for five years now and in that time he has given me a greater understanding as to the mental processes that take place on the golf course, both good and bad.

Not only has he helped me deal with the stresses that take place on the course but in life too. He has shown me how my tendencies on the golf course are very much related to my character and the state of mind off the course and that managing these will lead to better golf and a better way of life off the course.

I have no doubt that "The Now Golfer" will help people reach their full potential on and off the golf course.

Tim Clark, July 2012

# ACKNOWLEDGEMENT

This is a book for golfers – all golfers. It is not a treatise on Self-psychology Psychoanalysis, or the theory of brain and Mind.

It is an attempt to explain the basic mental principles that apply to the actual playing of the game of golf. In the author's opinion these are covert mental processes and inherent ones. To understand the correct principals is to allow the player a simpler mental awareness to playing a very complex and demanding game. The most important point underlying this book is to make golf more fun for the player.

I am completely convinced that a proper understanding of the right mental processes for playing golf will greatly increase your competency and pleasure. I guarantee that it will lessen the Tension and Anxiety that everyone experiences who plays this wonderful game.

Although we did not include footnotes in the text, there are a number of authors to whom I am deeply indebted. Foremost are the works of Heinz Kohut, the founder of the Self-psychology Psychoanalysis. There are many other authors who are deservedly important: Robert Stolorow, Wilma Gucci, Alan Shore, and Antonio Domasio, to name just a few.

Of course, the golfers are the ones who really taught me what happens in their Minds. I'm particularly grateful to

Ben Crane, Bo Van Pelt, Joe Durant, Grant Waite, and Jason Gore.

I am especially grateful to Stewart Cink for writing the Foreword, to Tim Clark for his Closing Thoughts, and to Martin Hall for his wonderful words in *The Journey*. I am also grateful to Mark Woods who first got me interested in working with professional golfers.

It has been and continues to be a tremendous pleasure and gift working with PGA professionals, both men and women. I have learned so much and continue to learn from these remarkable athletes. To me, golf is the greatest game there is. It elicits psychological challenges and tests that no other game presents. Golf truly reflects the greater inner drama of life. What a privilege it has been to work with those who have made it their life's work.

Pres Waddington - June, 2012

# GLOSSARY OF TERMS

Affect States – Refers to the feeling of experiencing an emotion. A state of being that is affected by a positive or negative emotion.

Anxiety – A state of uneasiness or apprehension, about future uncertainties. A psychological and physiological state that creates feelings of fear, worry, uneasiness, dread, and physical Tension. This mood condition often occurs without any identifiable triggering stimulus.

Aspirations – A strong desire to achieve something high or great. Aspirations differ from Expectations in that they are not tied to a personal sense of Self worth, but rather are goals a person wishes to strive for.

Big Picture – Refers to any and all elements of the inner and outer world that draw one's attention away from focusing on the task at hand or physically interferes with performance. Anything outside the Little Picture.

Expansive State - In or of a state characterized by an overestimation of one's Self, over-excitement, euphoria, and at times delusions of grandeur.

Expectations – The act of looking forward or anticipating. Expectations are goals that must be met in order to maintain Self-worth and are intrinsically tied to Self worth and

Self-esteem. Expectations are the killers of life and the golf swing.

Fight or Flight – An ingrained reaction to danger or the threat of danger, characterized by either fleeing to safety or standing to fight to survive. This reaction is built into human DNA and is often accompanied by accelerated heartbeat, dilation of pupils, secretion of adrenaline into the bloodstream, rapid breathing, and the involuntary tensing of muscles.

Guilt – A feeling or state of culpability stemming from committing a real or imagined offense. Guilt differs from Shame in that guilt seeks to rectify or be forgiven for said offense.

Healthy Narcissism – Healthy Narcissism is the desire to shine in the eyes of those people who represent the Ideal Other, and to value yourself in such a way that you feel that you are worthy of their admiration.

Ideal Other – The Ideal Other is a concept within a person's psyche who can be a single person, like a parent, or can be a conglomerate of people, like a person's family, friends, spouse, coaches, and idols...these valued individuals help form the ideals, norms, and aspirations that act as a compass to help guide a person through life.

Ideal Self – The way one wishes to perceive himself, based on the values, ideals, norms, and aspirations one chooses to make up the Ideal Other.

Implicit Procedural Memory System – The part of the Self originating from the Right Brain responsible for non-symbolic thought and spontaneous movements that have been ingrained into the Mind/body through training and repetition.

Little Picture - The concept of a person being totally in the Present moment, with Mind and body synchronized, free from the distractions caused by remembered events from the past and imagined events in the future, as well as being free from the physical Tension caused by expansive Affect States such as being overjoyed, or depletive Affect States such as Self-loathing.

Narcissism - The admiration of the Self by the Self.

Regulation - The act of controlling and maintaining one's thoughts and emotions when faced with events and traumas that cause de-regulation and Self-fragmentation. Regulation is the act of staying centered between the extremes of Self- depletion and Grandiosity.

Rhythmic Breathing - A type of conscious intentional breathing that facilitates the calming of the Self and the focusing of one's awareness on the Present and the attending awareness within the body.

Self - The combination of the Mind and the body and the resulting perception of the world as a result of that combination. The experience of "I AM".

Self Agency - Relying on the cohesiveness of one's Self to overcome deregulating traumas and the attending awareness to maintain that sense of Self-cohesion.

Self Cohesion - The ability to maintain or regulate one's mental and emotional states when faced with the traumas and pressures that tend to cause de-regulation and Self fragmentation.

Self Esteem – A measurement of one's Self, either in a positive or negative light. A way of regarding and experiencing one's Self.

Self Depletion – Regarding one's Self in a negative light and the resulting Vulnerability to Shame and other negative emotional states.

Shame – "A painful emotion caused by embarrassment, unworthiness, or disgrace," caused by a failure to live up to Expectations. Shame is a total body experience. If you feel Shamed, to you it means that your total person is defective, flawed, and inferior...and the response to Shame and the Vulnerability of Shame is to hide, to defend yourself at all costs against exposure as a flawed and inferior individual.

Time Traveling – The act of mentally leaving one's body, either into past memories or an imagined future.

# AUTHOR BIOS

**Dr. Preston L. Waddington, PHD, PA**, is a Psychoanalyst in private practice specializing in top athletes, particularly golfers, helping them to perform to their maximum potential under pressure. Pres is a member of the International Association of Self Psychology and is certified by Westchester Institute for Training in Psychotherapy and Psychoanalysis.

**Don Lay** is a former touring and teaching tennis professional. His students include the Kennedys, the Shrivers, Oleg Cassini, Peter Grace, Cliff Robertson, and Jimmy Buffett. Don's career on the tennis court, along with his background in psychology, has made him a lifetime student of how athletes learn, and how best to communicate this process.

# SPECIAL THANKS

Special thanks to Tracy Hanlon, for introducing me to the Master. To Cynthia McCahon for her wisdom and direction. To Chris Verna for sharing his knowledge and experience. To Bill Sewell for his support and sound advice. To Jennifer Holloway for her great artistic talents. To Karen Moran for her media expertise. And to Janet Lay for her editing and attention to all aspects of the publishing process. Also to Andy Timmerman Sr. for his eagle eye.

Don Lay, August, 2012

# PHOTO CREDITS

In order of appearance:

| | |
|---|---|
| #1. W.C. Fields - | mptvimages.com, D. Scott Chrisholm |
| #2. Ball on the Cup | 123rf.com |
| #3. Annika Sorenstam | AP Images |
| #4. Al Geiberger | AP Images |
| #5. Grandfather's Clock | Shutterstock Images LLC |
| #6. The Time Machine | mptvimages.com |
| #7. The Now Watch | Shutterstock Images LLC |
| #8. Little Girl Golfing | 123rf.com |
| #9 Past and Future | 123rf.com |
| #10 Golfer in a Dome | Shutterstock Images LLC |
| #11. Brain Hemispheres | Shutterstock Images LLC |
| #12. Swing Thoughts | 123rf.com |

| | |
|---|---|
| #13. Harry Vardon | AP Images |
| #14. Putting Swing Thoughts | Shutterstock Images LLC |
| #15. Buster Keaton Three Ages | mptvimages.com |
| #16. Narcissus | {PD} |
| #17. Mom and Baby | 123rf.com |
| #18. Ideal Other | Sister and astronaut –Shutterstock Images LLC |
| Little boy and flag and parents - Jack Nicklaus | 123rf.com AP Images |
| #19. White Heat | Getty Images, Allan Grant |
| #20. Grandiosity | Leaderboard, Rolls Royce, mansion, microphone, Golfer – Shutterstock Images |
| Applauding woman - | 123rf.com |
| #21. Jack Nicklaus | AP Images |
| #22. Man in the Dome (fleuron) | 123rf.com |

Made in the USA
San Bernardino, CA
13 December 2012